Justice

By

Sunny Frazier
Rick Smith
Nick Perna
Sherrill Swinney
Ian Snyder
David Kettering
Harriet Fox
Denise Spiller
Rick Tippins
Jim Padar
Jay Padar
C.L. Swinney

C.L.Swinney Publications
-2015-

~To the one hundred eighty six men and women who were killed in the line of duty in 2014, and those killed so far in 2015. To the thousands of military members who've perished in 2014 and into 2015. You gave the ultimate sacrifice, but rest assured it was not in vain. You'll be sorely missed, but never forgotten. Your watch has ended, but we'll continue to uphold our proud professions, push on with heavy hearts, until we too are called to our own end of watch.

Acknowledgements:

Cops Don't Cry, Shootout Prelude, Encounter, On The Fence, Have No Fear, The Police Are Here, and You Saved My Baby were previously printed in the novel, **On Being A Cop**, *December 2013 by On Being A Cop, LLC, which you can find* **here***.*

Thank you to the men and women who supported this project and submitted fantastic stories.

There may be offensive language in this collection of stories. At times, this type of language is necessary to communicate with folks who use it every day and to get a point across. The authors, and I, apologize to those the language may upset or offend.

Thank you to cover illustrator Bryan Keller for the amazing work he did getting this project together.

Table of Contents

Cops Don't Cry   8

That Look   14

Payback's a mother—cker: 16

Six Years In A Blur   22

Baby Blue (Fiction)   39

"You Saved My Baby!"   58

Have no fear, the police are here.   78

All I Ever Had (Fiction)   82

On the Fence   104

A Woman in a Man's World: Living inside a Correctional
Institution.   109

Shootout at the High Rollers Pool Hall: 124

Encounter   144

Forty-Three Minutes (Fiction)   151

Shooter   164

Forgotten Warriors   176

One Hundred Eighteen   181

Never Forget Our Fallen   185

Barometer   192

How Did I Get Here?   200

Ambush (Fiction)   212

Far From Routine (Fiction)   220

Contributor Biographies: 233

Cops Don't Cry

By Jim Padar

"For those of you here today who have a police officer as mother or father, know this;

At some time in their career they have come home from the street and wept for you."

-Father Thomas Nangle, Chicago Police Chaplain Family Day Mass, 2006.

1978, Homicide, Second Watch...

It was a beautiful warm summer day but the air was crisp, unencumbered by the awful humidity that sometimes grips Chicago in mid-August. Our sport coats hung in the back swaying gently as Mike Shull steered the unmarked sedan around the city's west side. Kids were everywhere. On bikes, playing baseball, and splashing in the occasional open hydrant.

Cops develop a background ear, constantly tuned to the drone of the radio. We were talking about nothing in particular, but immediately picked up our call when the dispatcher paged.

"Seventy-four-eleven."

I reached for the mic, "Seventy-four-eleven," I replied.

"Seventy-four-eleven, take the death investigation now at St. Mary's."

St. Mary's Hospital was a brand new hospital in a very old neighborhood. Brand new building, that is. The hospital had been there for generations but they had recently rebuilt. It was a modern state-of-the-art building. All private rooms, first class emergency room. Mike slid the car into a parking place reserved for police vehicles. We left our jackets in the car. No need to cover the revolver, handcuffs, ammo pouch. The hospital personnel knew us too well.

Inside we greeted the ER staff and they responded in subdued voices. It was a drowning. Male, white, about eight years old. He was removed from the bottom of the park pool by a life guard who administered CPR until the arrival of the Fire Ambulance. The paramedics continued CPR in route to the hospital. It's tough to give up on a kid. The ER doctor pronounced the boy dead on arrival. There must have been 200 kids in that pool, how long he was on the bottom was anyone's guess. Our job would be to eliminate foul play as a possible factor in the drowning. We gathered what little identifying information the hospital had and then headed to the examining room where he laid.

It could have been a scene from a movie. The heavy wood door with a large shaded glass swung open and on a gurney, under a sheet, was the

silhouette of a small human being. The nurse closed

the door behind us and Mike and I pulled the sheet

back. He looked to be about the reported age of

eight. Light brown curly hair, still wet. His turquoise

swim trunks clung to his pale white skin. My chest

gave an involuntary breath—no—a single convulsive

sob. My eyes welled and I turned away to compose

myself. The nurse was looking at me intently. Mike

never blinked. He continued with the examination of

the boy. Male, white, approximately 8 years of age,

brown hair, blue eyes, no bruises, no external signs of

violence. In less than a minute I returned to the

gurney, once again a stoic homicide detective. I

reached across, grasped his arm and pulled the cold,

wet little boy toward me. Mike scanned his backside

for any marks or indications of violence. No rigor, no

lividity, no bruises. We completed our notes and

returned to the nurses' station. They had received some additional information, possibly the location of his mother working as a waitress at a nearby restaurant. We would need another unit to get mother and bring her to the hospital for identification. Mike and I would go to the pool and interview the life guard and any witnesses.

Out in the lot we rolled down our car windows and paused for a moment to let the blast of now super-heated air out of the squad. Mike slid in behind the wheel. I waited for radio traffic to clear.

For the first time since the ER, Mike looked me in the eye. "You saw Craig, didn't you?"

"I did. I knew it wasn't him, but somehow I saw him lying on that gurney."

Cops try to keep their family separate from their street life. Most times they succeed. It's a necessity for mental survival. When you fail and identify family with a real life street scenario the results can be traumatic. My curly headed, brown eyed, eight-year-old was miles from here doing his summer thing, I felt sure of that.

The radio fell silent for a moment and I keyed the mike, "Seventy-four-eleven, we're going to need an assist car to locate the mother..."

That night as Craig raced into the house for supper, I grabbed him in a bear hug.

"Dad!" he shouted as he squirmed loose, "Cut it out!"

"Wash up!" I shouted after him with just a hint of a crack in my voice.

That Look

It happened again last night.
A toddler, well behaved and brave,
shed one single tear as he kissed
and hugged his "father," wearing handcuffs,
good bye. Years will pass before
physical contact might ensue.
Salty water fills my eyes, forcing
me to turn away. Mentally, I
try to fit into their shoes without
success. Pain and sorrow hangs in the air
like second-hand smoke searching
for lungs. Heartache crushes my spirit.
My programming is to serve and protect.
But I can't scoop him up, make the
pain, both his and mine, disappear.
I watch the "father" through sullied irises.
Palms to face, the gangster weeps,
but the little boy pauses, "It's okay daddy."
Formidable years, lost forever, since
jail visits and letters make terrible parents.

Damnit, now he looks at me,

asking with his soft eyes why I

want to take his daddy away?

Again I turn away. It's that look,

infuriating my heartburn far too often.

A glass full of poison greets my lips

when I'm alone. But I'm never really

alone. The voices don't stop. We

leave, heads hung low, pretending

like what we do truly matters.

-C. L. Swinney

Payback's a mother—cker:

The perils of working for free in law enforcement.

By Nick Perna

In the agency I work for, we're required to work one extra day a month for no extra pay. That's an additional 10 hours where you are basically working for free. They are called payback days and, I've learned over the years, payback's a motherfucker...

I had two very memorable experiences over two consecutive payback days a few years ago. On the first occasion, I was dispatched to a domestic disturbance in an apartment with another officer. For the unfamiliar, a domestic violence call can be a real pain in the ass for a beat cop. It almost always involves a lot of writing and is generally time intensive. The last thing you need when you are "donating" your time to the city is long call that makes you write a lot of paper.

My partner and I arrived and made the approach to a second story apartment. As we approached the door, I noticed it was slightly ajar. In an effort to avoid a lot of unnecessary paperwork by pushing the door open and actually viewing a domestic assault in progress, we opted to knock on the door to allow the involved parties to tidy themselves up. It's an old cop trick which has paid dividends over the years.

When you're on the job you learn to expect the unexpected. That being said, the unexpected is what you usually expect and this call did not disappoint. After a few knocks we heard what can be classified as a "ruckus" inside, people running around, and windows being pushed open quickly. At this point, we opened the door and were greeted by the oddest of sights: A young women with her arms bound behind her back with an extension cord. Me and my partner un-holstered our handguns and entered the apartment. In the bathroom, I located a young male also with his hands tied behind his back whose face showed the signs of a legitimate ass-whooping. He explained that he had been robbed, and that the crooks had pistol whipped him.

My partner and I soon realized that two criminals with handguns had been inside the apartment at the same time we were knocking on the door. Later, reflecting on it, we both realized it was what Steven King often describes as a "goose walking across your grave" moment. If I was a cat, I'd check the log to figure out how many of my nine lives I had left, and subtract one. We could have been killed trying to dodge paperwork...

We never caught the crooks, and the whole thing turned out to be a dope rip, which is a robbery to steal a drug dealer's drugs. Anyway, I made it to the end of the shift alive but bitter.

Fast forward to the very next payback day, this was a month later. I'm sent to a call of a big rig involved in an accident. When I got there, I found out that the truck had hit a power line, causing an outage for a city block. Live power lines were arcing in the street, creating a road hazard. It was rush hour so I wanted to clear the intersection fast. I went into the road where the power line was. I started directing traffic around it and began requesting an additional cop to help with traffic control.

As this was happening, another big rig drove past me in the opposite lane. The trailer of the truck connected with the downed power line. This caused the live wire to move rapidly, as if it was a fishing line being reeled in by an imaginary fishing reel.

Somehow the power line ended up between my feet. I first became aware of that fact when I felt the line rubbing against my leg. When I looked down, I saw the line moving rapidly between my legs, as it was being pulled by the trailer. I was on the radio as this all unfolded which caused me to swear on the radio, "Charles 4, I need another unit for traffic control. Can I get a unit at the corner of, SSSHHHIIITTT!"

I watched as the arcing wire moved closer to my legs, like a demonic snake with sparks as venom. I jumped straight up, it felt like I went about 10 feet in the air. For the older readers, I felt like the Rayovac cat, you know, the one pictured on the side of the battery. The arcing end literally missed me by inches.

It most likely would have been the end of my career, if not my life, if that thing had connected with me.

I pride myself on my ability to quickly react to situations on the street. I've been through foot pursuits, fist fights, gun fights, and just about every other type of in-progress call you can imagine. But, the arcing wire of death left me speechless. I kind of checked out for a couple of seconds as I realized I could probably check off another "cat life." When I came to, I realized that I heard the sounds of police sirens in the background. The last thing dispatch had heard from me was an "S-bomb" expletive followed by a lot of silence. I quickly got on the radio and said everything was cool and to slow down the cavalry.

In the span of a few months, I almost got my ticket punched twice, while working for free. As I said, payback's a motherfucker...

Six Years In A Blur

By C.L.Swinney

The phone call from the sergeant advising me the Narcotics Task Force (NTF), the most coveted and bad-ass spot in the entire office (accept for SWAT, but I didn't make the height requirement for that team), was the highlight of my career.

On the first day, my training officer had me write two search warrants, the first two I ever wrote, which we served the same day too. Senior guys in the group raised their eyebrows noticing how quickly I typed and how eager I was to kick ass. Things happened so quickly I missed the initial hazing period, but those days would follow.

Before long, I was set free of my training officer and intended to be the best Narc in the state. My vision was to single-handedly win the war on drugs. However, the ugly sin of jealousy reared its sour head and my first "bump" was encountered.

It turns out, many in my office didn't think I deserved to get the spot, and some secretly hoped I would fail and be banished to some lowly spot in the office. In fact, two fellow co-workers were told specifically that they were a shoe-in for the two spots available. Neither of them made it. I guess I tested better, and had whatever it was the administration wanted because I placed number one on the list. However, cops are fragile, and because these individuals were passed, I became enemy number one. That bothered me, and still bothers me today, but, once a cop makes up his or her mind, there's no changing it. We bring stubborn to a whole new level.

I tried to shield myself from the in-house drama (picture police departments a lot like high-school cool kid contests) and immersed myself in as many cases as possible- partly to keep my mind off things, and partly to learn. Within six months, I'd done almost every kind of case possible, including working undercover.

Then, while I strutted around like I owned the place, I was asked if I would take a spot at a Task Force ran by the California Department of Justice, Bureau of Narcotics (now defunct). When a lieutenant asks for a favor, you never say no. So, I reported to the Task Force and started a whole new chapter as a narcotics investigator, this time cross-designated as a state agent.

As far as cases go, I went from having my confidential informants (CI) buying grams of crystal methamphetamine or some other illegal drug, gathering enough probable cause to obtain a search warrant, and hitting a suspect's house, to my CI's purchasing quarter or half-pounds of narcotics and stretching investigations for months, even years. We didn't look for the street dealer, we wanted their suppliers. In order to accomplish this, we needed much more money (we call it buy-funds), which the state (at the time) had. The goal was to work a case until it could go no further, then try to convince federal agents (DEA, HSI) to adopt the case and work a wiretap(s).

I wrote seven wiretaps while assigned to the DOJ Task Force. Doesn't sound like a lot, but consider each affidavit was approximately 140-200 pages (Microsoft word, 12-point font). These were followed by ten day reports, daily phone call logs, daily surveillance reports, buy reports, interception reports, and all the other stuff that happens throughout a wiretap investigation. I figure I wrote thousands of pages during these cases, but, beyond the twenty-four work days, no weekends off, no time with the family, no holidays off, sifting through thousands of calls, and handling case emergencies, it was still worth it.

Listening to people talk, what they say and how they say it, and what they truly think, is eerie. Imagine all the emails, texts, or conversations you've had with friends, family, or strangers that you would freak out if someone else heard them. It's pretty crazy.

In one of my cases, I heard my primary suspect and his friend talking about doing a "lick," slang for robbery. They talked about doing "licks" often, but this one seemed like it wasn't going to actually happen, so I dismissed it. By dismissing it, I mean I didn't let anyone else know they were talking about it. I could do that because I was the Case Agent (who is always right and if you don't like it, get off my case).

About three hours later, my primary target made an outgoing call. He was using the old push-to-talk Sprint cell phone function. I heard a woman screaming and my primary target scream, "Get the fucking car! Shit, someone's here!"

Another person, different than who my target was talking to earlier in the day, frantically answered, "Shit dog! Get the fuck out, they coming!"

My heart pounded as I waited for the necessary data to come through so I could figure out where these monsters were and send the local police to help the victim. There was no doubt in my mind that they were burglarizing a home and found the home owner inside while doing so. Two things normally happen in these scenarios, the suspect(s) flee, or they do something drastic to the victim because they are scared or boxed in like an animal.

After what felt like an eternity, I was able to figure out precisely where the event was happening and called the appropriate dispatch center and asked them to send units code three (full lights and sirens) to the house. The Redwood City Police Department responded quickly, and sure as heck, they found two suspects running from the area I told them to look. The suspects were wearing all-black clothing and had push-to-talk cell phones. They were detained and the victim was contacted...she was okay, accept for the fact she was scared out of her mind while waking up to burglars rummaging through her home.

I stayed in the wire room and had to make a decision, do I let the suspects go or have them arrested? Sounds strange, doesn't it? Most cops would automatically say arrest those guys. However, would I gain more by letting them go and intercept my primary target and his friends discussing the robbery? Tough call, right? If my primary target was arrested, the wiretap would end (at the time the wire was in the beginning and we didn't have enough to pin a case on any of the suspects). I knew I could build an even stronger case against the suspects and seek an arrest warrant for them later. The woman's initial scream; however, caused chills to run down my back. Either way, it was a judgment call I wasn't prepared for, and at the time, I wanted nothing to do with it. Ultimately, I told the officers on scene to let the suspects go.

I still don't know if it was the right call, but, the wiretap went on for almost six more months. By letting the case continue, we were able to solve seven residential burglaries (and charge three people with the burglary mentioned above), we seized twelve guns, one and a half kilos of heroin, and completely dismantled a gang who'd been terrorizing law enforcement and local communities for ten years. To this day, I hear the victim's scream at night. We never met, but with the help of the Santa Clara County District Attorney's Office (and many other agencies), the people responsible for her grief were sent to prison for a long time.

Then further change occurred. The task force I was in, at first eight members strong, dwindled down to two people, me and the Task Force Commander. Essentially, the California Governor went after DOJ and specifically the Bureau of Narcotic Enforcement. Friends of mine were laid off or relocated. It was a rough time for me. I already made more money than they did and I could get overtime, but these guys were taking it on the chin, some with ten years on. BNE was the longest running narcotics task force in California, maybe even the US, until then.

Suddenly, narcotic cases were no longer important, and our focus turned to guns and gang members. I have no problem taking them on, so I adapted quickly. Before long, I was assisting the San Jose Police Department, and many other agencies, with armed robbery and homicide cases (we also did abduction and kidnapping cases). It was a big shift, but a case is a case. If you handle the nuts and bolts of the investigation the same every time, you'll be successful the majority of the time. I embraced this change and was later given a partner from the San Jose Police Department. Together, along with the Homicide Division and others who cannot be mentioned, we worked hundreds of homicides, bank robberies, rapes, kidnapping, and child abduction cases.

I cannot, and will not, go into details about how we located these suspects, but I can tell you we apprehended all but three of them (at the time). One guy killed himself after molesting his daughter (we found him, but the coward ended his own life instead of facing his charges like a man), and two fled to Mexico. One of them was taken into custody recently. He's sitting in the Santa Clara County jail facing a murder charge. The other, well, he's gonna meet some of my friends real soon...

As these cases continued, my Task Force Commander surprised everyone and announced his retirement. My partner went back to San Jose Police Department, and I merged into another DOJ group in the same building. My focus again changed. I worked undercover at rave concerts, as a "John" for massage parlors, and assisted with a homicide wiretap which resulted in four suspects being arrested and charged with the murder of a defenseless store clerk over some swisher sweets and about a hundred dollars (unreal what some people will do or are capable of).

Undercover work is challenging and can be scary. I'd say I was more excited than scared, but if you don't have the "oh crap" radar constantly going, you shouldn't work undercover. I quickly learned my specialty was dressing up in silly costumes, the kind that will undoubtedly come out as photos at a retirement party, and purchasing ecstasy or other club drugs from dealers. For some reason, the suspects loved me.

Working with an arrest team at these wild events was satisfying because one year, at the Cow Palace, we worked an event where two kids died. We initially thought they'd taken "bad" pills, but it turned out, the pills they took were extremely pure and proved too much for their hearts and internal organs. That's why we worked those events, amazing how the public outcry (the promoter of such events) lessens when teenagers die. Dead children never become routine, and my heart never stops aching.

When I see a dead person, especially a child, a piece of me dies with them. It bothers me constantly. I can recall every single dead body I've seen in the last thirteen years. I wish the images would disappear, but they won't. If that's how I feel, imagine how the friends and family of the deceased feel? Compassion goes a long way in this line of work, yet many of the people who wear a badge have a difficult time understanding that.

Anyway, I would stay at the DOJ Task Force for almost five years total. In the end, it was time for me to go. Ballyhoo was afoot, but I sure miss my old team.

I went back to NTF and had hoped to remain there as long as I could. I'd worked out the shifts and time constraints with my wife and the kids, and we were doing pretty well. I always told my wife if the assignment I was in was too much for her, I'd find a new spot. She never asked me to do so, although I know she wanted to.

I gave NTF six years of my life, some of the best years of my career, but recently I was rotated back to patrol. I lost the detective title and the pay, and it took me almost two weeks to swallow that pill. I'm over it now, finally.

I thought patrol would be easier, with a set schedule and all, but the recent events around the United States, specifically two NYPD officers being murdered, have put my mind into over-drive. I can't stay parked in one spot too long. I constantly look at people and mentally rehearse (and assume) that they are armed, and want to kill me. I don't let my guard down during my entire 12-hour shift. I have headaches, and my eyes burn. The tragic events that have happened around our country replay in my head repeatedly. Family and friends support me, yet others do not, and it's clear they do not care for police. Somehow they lump one bad cop into all of us being bad. I've seen the looks in people's eyes these days; people are unhappy and are willing to kill a cop to demonstrate that point.

What I learned during these six years is this. I chose this job, but in some way, I feel it called to me. I will continue to wear the badge proudly, and do my best to serve the community I work for. I will strive to be as respectful and professional as I can to each and every person I come into contact with. I acknowledge that people want change, and mistakes have been made. I've made mistakes too, not big ones, but I've made them.

Nevertheless, I promised my fellow co-workers and to everyone wearing a badge, as well as every member in the community, that I would protect and serve them. While the kinks of our profession are digested and addressed, by committees created across the nation (and the President of the United States), I expect people I contact to act like human beings and treat me fairly. I'm not the person who did the things you perceive as wrong, so don't take out your issues on me. If I do something you feel is disrespectful, tell me and we can talk it out like adults. Often times, you'll find that I'll apologize when I'm wrong. The social glue of our society weakens by the day, and if we can't find a way to work together, things will continue to get worse before they get better. Remember that even after all the negativity, and the murders of men and women in blue, we're still prepared to sacrifice our lives to rescue you...even though we know we could die at any time. It's what we do, and we love doing it.

Baby Blue (Fiction)

By Sunny Frazier

Foreword: "Forensics Files" (8 p.m., Court TV), police find vital evidence in a vacuum cleaner bag kept in storage for 24 years.

The 1962 abduction and murder of 15-year-old Marlene Miller shocked the rural community of Hanford, outside of Fresno, Calif. Police quickly found circumstantial evidence tying nearby farm worker and onetime convicted rapist Booker T. Hillery to the crime scene.

After a jury convicted him of murder and sentenced him to death, Hillery used every appeal at his disposal. In the 1970s, the Supreme Court struck down the death penalty. By the 1980s, a court found that Hillery's grand jury might have been racially prejudiced and ordered a new trial.

Rather than base their case on 24-year-old testimony from witnesses who had long since died, prosecutors decided to take a new look at existing evidence using advanced technology. This is where the old vacuum cleaner bag came in handy. Inside, police found tiny white blobs that they couldn't explain back in 1962. By 1986, experts could identify them as microscopic drops formed when aerosol spray paint clung to fabric. Apparently, Miller's killer left a nearly invisible trail of such globs all over the carpet.

Amazingly, Hanford police still had Hillery's Plymouth in storage. And a quick look at the old heap revealed that someone had tried to redecorate the inside roof of the car using spray paint. Faced with this new evidence, a jury had no trouble re-convicting Hillery.

BABY BLUE

People in the rural California community of Hanford clearly remembered the 1961 case. The murder of Amy Monroe convinced farmers to put security locks on their doors and keep their daughters close by. Forty-seven years had passed, but memories stirred every time Edward Jensen came up for parole.

I carried the forms in a leather briefcase, a gift from my parents when I graduated from the police academy in 1967. There were few women in the ranks back then, and I didn't use the case much except when I testified in court. Now that I'd been shunted off to administration, the aging briefcase was filled with busy work from the sheriff. Nobody called me dead weight to my face, but menial tasks found their way to my desk. The brass felt they had to justify my position until I retired.

I badged the guard and put my car keys in the holding tray. I hadn't carried a service weapon since my glaucoma surgery. The sentry buzzed me through the prison door with a two finger salute and a respectful "Ma'am." My rank of sergeant went unnoticed.

Coalinga State Prison is a series of massive gray cubes behind layers of barbed concertina wire. The desolated rolling hills, already marred by discarded oil rigs, were no worse off with the addition of concrete landscape.

Jensen sat in the interview room. The shackles and guard were reassuring, at least for me. The twenty-two year old kid who had raped and brutally murdered Amy Monroe looked hostile in his mug shot. Now Jensen's face was etched with uncompromised evil.

"Are you with the Parole Board?"

I didn't answer, just slipped into the seat across from him and set down the briefcase.

"I'm just the person tying up loose ends." I flipped papers until I came to his file.

Jensen glanced from me to the guard standing at parade rest in front of the door.

"I'm not a lawyer, Mr. Jensen. The guard stays."

He shrugged and slouched in his seat, already bored with my visit.

"I'm here because you requested that your 1958 Buick remain in the county evidence yard."

"It's a classic now." Jensen straightened up; proud that he owned something of value.

"The problem is, Mr. Jensen, the county holding facility is being torn down to make way for a freeway. We're transferring property to a new site. Your car doesn't run and is in bad condition from sitting outside for over forty years. I have paperwork for you to sign releasing the county from responsibility of the vehicle. We can tow the car to a location of your choice, or send it to a scrap metal yard."

"Nope." Jensen was smug with his minor victory.

"You haven't paid a penny for storage," I pointed out.

"The sheriff put my car in the lock-up. I got the right to have my ride waiting for me when I get out." He grinned, displaying a sad lack of prison dental care. "Maybe I'll take you joy riding. Would you like that?"

I ignored him and pulled out another piece of paperwork from the ledger. "In that case, I need your signature authorizing us to transport the vehicle to the new yard."

"I call her Baby Blue," he confided as he awkwardly picked up the pen in his left hand and scrawled his name on the document.

I slid the document back in the folder and nodded to him. Business was done between us.

"You take care of my baby," Jensen crooned. "Tell her I'll be coming soon."

*****

For this parole hearing, Jensen had a sharp lawyer and a real chance of getting out. Evidence in the original case was solid at the time of the trial, but advances in DNA had the judicial system looking hard at all capital cases.

I'd read the Murder Book on the Jensen case so many times, the crime played out like a movie in my head. Scene: A warm Friday night in late May. At seven o'clock, the Monroe family leaves for the Starlight Drive-In to see "Gidget Goes To Rome."

Sixteen-year-old Amy stays home to finish sewing her prom dress. It's a warm night, the windows are open to catch the breezes. The door is unlocked, normal for a rural farmhouse.

At approximately 9:30 p.m., the family returns home. The room where Amy was sewing is in shambles. The Singer sewing machine is overturned, fabric and spools of thread are spilled out on the carpet. A pair of sewing scissors have blood residue. Amy Monroe is missing.

At 10 p.m., Kings County Sheriff's Deputies are dispatched to the Monroe home. Statements are taken from the family, but only a cursory search of the perimeter is done. A full search is delayed until daylight. Checks are made by phone to area hospitals and clinics.

At 6 a.m. Saturday morning, sheriff's deputies conduct an extended search around the area of the

Monroe ranch. The partially nude body of Amy Monroe is found in a dry irrigation canal. There are indications of rape and eight stab wounds. A cast is made of tire tracks at the scene. Boot prints are visible.

Twenty-two year old Edward Jensen, a mechanic who lives twelve miles from the Monroe's, is picked up for questioning. Jensen has a juvenile record for statutory rape and priors for battery. Witnesses state they saw a light blue Buick Riviera parked on 13th Avenue the night of the murder. Based on shoe prints and tire tracks found at both crime scenes, statements by witnesses, plus juvenile records showing a predisposition to criminal action, the jury convicts Jensen for First Degree Murder. The sentence is life.

That was then. This is now, and Jensen's latest defense attorney, a hot shot from Santa Barbara, had his sights set on making the climb to DA. The admission of Jensen's juvenile records at trial was hotly disputed. Rape kits didn't exist in the early '60's, so there would be no last minute DNA reveals. The defense claimed the ruling was based on circumstantial evidence and a biased jury. Jensen had a good shot at walking away a free man and the county would have another lawsuit on the books.

I wanted to care more, but it was an old case. My problem was moving the hulk of a rusted auto to the new yard. Any reasonable man would have signed off on the junk heap years ago. Jensen never intended to play nice with the county. He knew his rights, and one of them was storage of property until his release or death. He probably got some pleasure from sticking the bill to Kings County.

*****

The impound lot was hot and dusty. Most of the cars were towed to the yard after DUI arrests. I spotted interior side panels stacked against the rear wheel of a Caddie. That would be Tuesday's drug bust. Crime tape isolated an SUV where a corpse was stashed less than a week ago.

The Riviera sat in the far corner of the yard. Years of dust layered the robin-egg blue paint job. The grill work was rusted out. The muscle car had gone to seed, just like the owner.

My partner and I drank from water bottles as we waited for the tow truck. I was fine under the spare shade of a drought-starved oak, but my partner couldn't stay still. He circled the Buick twice before he called to me, "Fran, come and look at this."

He pointed to the interior of the car. The passenger door was rusted open. Weather damage had eaten through the floor boards and rotted upholstery dangled down over the seats. But that wasn't what grabbed my partner's interest. It was the God-awful color.

There was a frustrated interior decorator somewhere in Jensen's psyche. He'd taken the Baby Blue theme to the next level by color-coordinating his beloved car. The inside matched the outside of the Riviera.

"Who the hell does this to their ride?" my partner said, choking on laughter. "You're older than me, so 'fess up—is this some sort of psychedelic sixties trend I'm lookin' at?"

I gave him a shove for bringing up the age difference.

I wanted a closer look at the inside, but didn't want to fight the spider webs connecting shredded cloth to the frame. After several hard tugs, I got the rear door open. A cloud of dust escaped. I covered my nose and mouth and waved the debris away.

Blue paint, grayed by age, covered the sides, seats, flooring, ashtrays, everything in the car. The paint job was cracked and peeling. I slipped a fingernail under a shard and flicked it off.

"The idiot spray painted the inside of his car," I said in disbelief.

"Before or after he was high on the fumes?"

Scattered on the floor were tiny balls, the size of sprinkles that decorate cupcakes. Upon closer inspection, I could see they were actually tear-drop shaped, not round. They mixed with the dust I stirred up when I opened the door, but were too heavy to stay airborne. My uniform was covered with the specks.

"The tow-truck's at the gate," my partner informed me.

"The Buick's not going anywhere," I answered.

I pulled rank, ignored my partner's protests and the middle-finger flip from the tow truck driver. I headed back to headquarters.

*****

Back in the office, I took the Murder Book from the case shelf. I let my partner deal with the lieutenant, who'd already gotten an earful from the tow yard.

There wasn't much listed on the evidence sheet. Good for the defense attorney, bad for the parole hearing. I scanned the faded carbon typeface, looking for the phrase that barely registered when I initially went over the paperwork.

ITEM 23. HOOVER VACUUM BAG.

Forensic science, even in infancy form, didn't exist until the seventies. Crime scenes were routinely compromised by homicide investigators. I knew detectives in the early years of my career who stubbornly resisted changes in police protocol. Hell, they even smoked on-site, discarding butts a few feet away from the corpse.

But, someone on the homicide crew had enough common sense to vacuum the crime scene. According to the report, Mrs. Monroe had vacuumed the room the same afternoon as the murder. The investigator used the Hoover owned by the family after inserting a fresh bag. The action was listed almost as a footnote: "Vacuumed crime scene floor and rug. Contents sealed in vacuum bag, Item #23."

I called over to the evidence room and gave the deputy on duty the year, case number and evidence number. He asked me to repeat the numbers three times. "What am I looking for, exactly?"

"A vacuum bag. Hoover model."

"You expect to find something like that after forty years? I don't even know where to begin looking."

My lieutenant tried to sideline me for an explanation of the tow incident. I ignored him and let my partner take the flack. I drove across town to the storage facility. The deputy had no problem bending the rules to save himself work. He buzzed me in and waved me off toward the far side of the building.

Hiking through a maze of metal racks filled to the ceiling with boxes in what passed for order, I tried to find my way. Signs were randomly posted counting down the years. I edged past the eighties, stumbled through the seventies, and finally found a small cache of sixties' evidence. Items were bagged and tagged, although the ink was smeared and illegible on many evidence envelopes.

The vacuum bag was wrapped in plastic and squashed behind something that looked like an old radio. I carefully fished out the package. The seal had held over the years. There were no signs of leakage. Gotta give it to duct tape.

Signing out the evidence meant phone calls, raising red flags throughout headquarters. I had an unwelcoming committee waiting for me. The homicide lieutenant, DA, my partner, and the sheriff were skeptical. My actions were going to be upgraded from insubordination to dementia.

We trooped into the forensic lab and handed the vacuum bag over to the experts.

Dirt, fibers, threads and hairs were sifted out of the bag. Sprinkled throughout the debris were small, baby-blue paint balls. They matched the tear-drop paint in the plasticine bag that I'd taken from the vehicle. The evidence put Jensen in the sewing room on the day of the murder.

The board didn't have a problem denying parole. Jensen's lawyer still tried to argue contamination of the chain of evidence and the possibility that a passenger tracked in the paint. The straws he grasped poked more holes in Jensen's alibi that he'd been in Bakersfield during the week of the murder. Maybe in this case a life sentence would really mean life.

I was given a grudging nod for my good work from the sheriff, but not much gratitude backed up the gesture. The forensic crew took me out for beers and we toasted Jensen's idiocy. Spray painting the inside of a car was one for the books. By refusing to sign off Baby Blue's release to the auto graveyard, Jensen's fate was as tightly sealed as the Hoover bag. Time was a foe to be respected.

I filed my retirement papers the next day.

"You Saved My Baby!”

By Jim Padar

Chicago's West Side, 1975. The radio call was a man stabbed.

Mike and I trotted in between the buildings of the Henry Horner Homes, but we instinctively slowed approaching the play lot. There was a crowd as one would expect on this warm summer evening especially at the scene of a stabbing—but the people were strangely quiet—there was clearly something else going on here. Just a few months earlier a Chicago Police Officer had been shot and killed by a sniper from these buildings. It was not a nice place to be, and tonight we were the first officers on the scene.

We slowed and unsnapped our holsters, keeping our hands on our snub nose revolvers as we continued more cautiously toward the group. Our uniform was "summer homicide," short sleeve dress shirts, ties and slacks. Our sport coats hung on the rear seat hooks in our unmarked sedan now parked at the curb on the south edge of the housing project. Our lifeline, our radio, was firmly affixed to the dashboard of the car; the Detective Division would be the last in the department to be upgraded to the new handheld personal radios.

As we got closer, the crowd took note and created a path for us. In the center of the group lay a muscular teen-ager, staring wide eyed at the sky. No one was within 20 feet of him and we stopped in our tracks when we saw why. The shirtless young black male had been stabbed in the neck—the right carotid artery to be exact—and with each contraction of his heart a stream of blood shot 10 to 15 feet from his body. He writhed about from time to time and the direction of the blood would shift slightly with each movement. The crowd would murmur and shift even further away. We snapped our holster straps closed.

"Oh shit!" Mike and I exclaimed simultaneously. No matter how many first aid movies you may have seen, nothing can prepare you for this sight in real life.

"I'll get a compress," said Mike as he headed back to the car.

"And call for an ambulance!" I yelled after him as I approached the young man.

In our police careers both Mike and I had witnessed people bleed out from massive head wounds or other horrendous trauma that simply could not be staunched with the 4" gauze compresses we carried in our case. But this was different. The point of bleeding was immediately identifiable. If I could just get my fingers on that point and apply pressure until Mike retuned, he might have a chance. I wasn't quite sure how we would apply a compress with enough pressure and avoid strangling the young man at the same time, but that was not the present problem.

Somehow I got close enough to his body without getting a direct hit. I knelt next to him and placed the fingers of my right hand directly on the wound. I could feel the carotid pulsing but miraculously the bleeding stopped. With that accomplished I had time to contemplate our next move, but I didn't have the faintest idea what that would be. I looked at his face, still wide eyed but conscious. Primal fear was the only way to describe his expression. The crowd stared silently. In the background I could hear the wail of responding sirens. What seemed like several minutes was in reality probably only seconds.

Mike, 12th District uniform personnel and two paramedics burst through the crowd at the same time... and they stopped in their tracks.

"Oh shit," said the paramedics as they looked at streams of blood spatter that had streaked across the concrete.

"No shit," I muttered to myself.

They showed a light on the man's neck and my hand.

"Don't move your hand!" they said as they opened their case of magic.

"Flatten your palm against his neck, but don't move your fingers. Pressure! Maintain pressure!"

Okay I'm doing that I thought to myself.

Imagine my surprise when their magic appeared to be yards and yards of Ace bandages wrapped around my hand and the victim's neck.

"And your plan is?" I asked

"You're coming with us," they said. "And don't move your fingers!"

One of the paramedics retreated to the ambulance and returned with the stretcher. It wasn't easy but somehow they maneuvered the patient, now totally unconscious, onto the stretcher, raised it to about waist high and all of us began to glide slowly toward the street. Once at the ambulance it was apparent that I was on the wrong side for conventional transport.

"You'll have to kneel next to him."

I looked at the corrugated steel floor. "Not without a pillow."

"Give the pussy a pillow," said one of the paramedics with a glint in his eye.

"Don't fuck with me or I'll move my fingers."

"Okay, okay!"

Once inside the ambulance it was all business. The one paramedic started oxygen and was attempting to start an IV line while the other was radioing vital signs to the hospital. It was the first time I recall hearing the term "hypovolemic shock" amongst other medical terms and the hospital responded in a terse exchange with the paramedic on the radio.

The silent crowd had come alive and surrounded our vehicle and began pounding on the sides.

"What choo doin?"

"Ain't you goin a take em?"

"Go! Go! Go!" They began to chant, all the while pounding on the sides of the ambulance.

The paramedic was still struggling with the IV.

A blue and white checkered hat appeared at the sliding window on the rear door.

"Hey guys, ya gotta move. There's too many of them here."

"Godammit!" cursed the paramedic on the radio.

"Stand-by, we have to move!" he shouted into the radio.

He climbed into the driver's seat and we sped a few blocks to a parking lot on the far side of the Chicago Stadium.

"If we don't get an IV started we're going to lose him." he said as he climbed back with us.

"Negative on the IV" ordered the hospital. "Transport stat!"

"Give me five more seconds," said the paramedic next to me.

And then miraculously, "Got it!"

"Let's move!"

I had never ridden in anything other than an old fashioned Cadillac ambulance and was astounded to observe that the newer ambulances were built on a truck chassis. Every block of our ride reminded me of that fact.

At the back door of County we once again had to gyrate and contort to get the two of us out of the ambulance, my right hand and his neck remaining securely fastened together. That accomplished we snaked our way through the corridor of the Emergency Room—which strangely was not our destination. We rolled out into the hallway where an elevator took us to the second floor Trauma Unit known simply as Ward 32. I had been there dozens of times investigating various shooting and stabbings. The Cook County Trauma Unit was probably one of the most competent in the world, but this visit would be quite different for me.

If I thought the patient and I were to be immediately released from one another I was mistaken. The paramedics described the incredulous scene to the doctors and they turned to me questioningly.

"That's right," I said, "He was pumping 10 to 15 foot streams."

"And that's where your fingers are now?"

I nodded.

"Don't move your hand."

And they started to work their medical magic. The victim was smoothly transferred from the fire department stretcher to the trauma unit gurney. His blood pressure was perilously low, called out with a single number rather than the pair of figures we are used to hearing. "Sixty!" And a few moments later, "Fifty-five!" Pulse was rapid. There were no breath sounds in his right lung. A urinary catheter was inserted—that always caused me to shudder no matter how many times I had seen the procedure. They couldn't start their own IV and the one started in the parking lot of the Chicago Stadium was now being used to push a unit of blood while they started a cut down in his groin to provide for a more rapid infusion of blood.

At any given moment there were four or more persons working on him, the medical terms being thrown about by doctors and nurses alike sounded like foreign language to me. I understood enough to know that they suspected that internal bleeding may have drained into his plural cavity causing the right lung to collapse. They called for a chest tube to be inserted immediately next to where my right elbow was positioned. I shifted away a few inches, but I couldn't move any further. The incision and insertion without anesthetic resulted in a low moan and some movement on the patient's part and I took that as an encouraging sign. But when the tube was finally inserted bright red blood flowed out, confirming internal bleeding.

"Clamp it! Clamp it!" someone shouted. "We need to get more blood into him."

Every step was a balancing act but slowly I began to get the general impression that the plan was to prepare him for transport to the operating room. A vascular surgery team had been assembled and was in place. How far would I go, I wondered silently.

Suddenly they were concentrating on the ace bandages around my hand and his neck.

"Don't move your hand until we tell you!" Maintain pressure!"

They started to unwrap several feet of blood soaked elastic bandages.

"Okay... when we tell you... remove your hand and step away."

I checked the path behind me and nodded my head.

"Now!" shouted the doctor.

I pulled my hand away and stepped into the pathway behind me without looking back at the patient. We had been joined together for well over an hour. As I flexed my hand and elbow, he and his gurney were disappearing out the door on the way to the OR. I found a wash station at the back of the Trauma Unit and scrubbed with a Hexachlorophene impregnated sponge for several minutes. While I was drying, Mike appeared at my side.

"Where's that 4" compress I sent you for?" I said with mock indignation.

"Go fuck yourself," he responded. "Can we leave now, doctor?"

We laughed and the medical people still in the trauma unit shot us a look.

I had blood on my shirt and I was sure there had to be some on my trousers. We only had about 90 minutes left on our shift.

"Let's go in to the office. I'm going to ask to be excused so I can go home and cleanup. Do we have any idea who this guy is?"

"I know who he is," said Mike facetiously. "Wiggins. Larry Wiggins. He's 19 and he lives in the Henry Horner Homes."

"Well I'm glad you were doing something useful while I was... tied up." We both laughed again.

Back at our Maxwell Street office, Mike started typing a Serafini Report, an unofficial note detailing what we knew, in the event Wiggins expired before we returned to work the next afternoon.

I headed home to shower and throw in a load of laundry.

*****

For the next two days we immediately checked on Larry Wiggins' condition when we arrived for work. The first day post-op they carried him as "critical." The second day he got a half notch upgrade to "critical but stable," a meager improvement.

We attempted some interviews at the Henry Horner Homes but the attitude toward the police was several steps beyond hostile. The offender was nick-named "Pookie" and we got a general physical description, but nobody would identify him beyond that. We enlisted the help of a robbery detective from our adjoining office. He was an encyclopedia of ghetto nicknames. Problem was, he told us, there were about a dozen Pookies on the west side. But with Larry Wiggins very slowly improving, he began to drop lower on our priority list. Homicide was the game and our Maxwell Street unit had earned the nickname "The Murder Factory" the hard way. Wiggins was alive and improving—time enough to interview him in person in a week or so.

The third day when we arrived for work, there was no need to call the hospital. The sergeant handed us a report from our morgue man reclassifying the Wiggins Aggravated Battery to Homicide/Murder. Larry Wiggins had expired suddenly during the early morning hours. The autopsy listed his cause of death as "Cerebral Thrombosis secondary to Traumatic Laceration of the Right Carotid Artery (Stab Wound). In short, Larry had suffered a stroke from a blood clot that had probably originated from the site of the knife wound. That put Larry back at the top of our priority list for the evening.

After roll call we trekked over to the Henry Horner Homes once again, but this time we went directly to the apartment where Larry had lived with his mother and sisters. As we entered, the mood was quiet and somber. A girl I would later learn was Larry's younger sister turned to her mother.

"Mama, this is the detective I told you about," as she nodded toward me.

"Oh sweet Jesus!" she shouted as she took about three steps and put me in a bear hug. "You saved my baby! You saved my baby!" She sobbed as she held tight to me.

Didn't she know? Hadn't they told her? Her son had been dead now for well over 12 hours. I held her tight, not knowing what her reaction was going to be, but she had to know the truth.

"Ma'am! Ma'am!" I put my mouth close to her ear. "Larry passed away early this morning."

She released me and put her hands on each of my arms just above the elbow.

"Don't you understand?" she said. "You gave him a chance, oh Lord, you gave him a chance!"

I stared dumbly at her as she regained her composure.

"Jesus put you there so we would could see him and tell him we loved him... and say good-bye. You did that for us."

"Yes ma'am," was all I could say.

"We're looking for Pookie," I added lamely after a short pause.

She stood straighter and stronger, taking on the persona of the tough, resilient black matriarchs that I had seen so often in the ghetto.

"We know Pookie," she said. "We'll bring him in to you."

"Mrs. Wiggins, that's our job. We don't want anything happening to you... or to Pookie."

She smiled, indulgently I thought.

"His mama and I—we bring him in to you—ain't nothin' goin to happen to him. We be doin' the right thing." Her tone left no room for argument.

Two hours later an entourage arrived at the Maxwell Street Homicide office with Pookie in tow. He was a big young man, but with his mama at his side he looked meek and bedraggled. They stayed at the office while we took statements from Pookie and several witnesses. The Assistant State's Attorney from the Felony Review Unit arrived, reviewed the case and approved murder charges.

It was well after midnight when we called for Pookie to be transported to the lock-up. The two mamas, Larry's sisters and two witnesses left together. Everybody's lives had changed the past few days, but the mamas walked out arm in arm, solid and straight. In a very real sense, they had each lost a son to ghetto violence, but no pair of mothers ever appeared more resolute in adversity.

I should have felt good... investigation... arrest... a cleared homicide... but in one way it was a hollow accomplishment—I really hadn't "saved" anybody.

Have no fear, the police are here.

By Jay Padar

It was a simple call, very routine.

"Twenty-four-twelve."

"Two-four-one-two."

"Twenty-four-twelve, see Mr. Mohammed regarding someone knocking at his rear window. He stated someone broke that same window last week and he's afraid that they're back."

"Twenty-four-twelve—ten-four—on our way squad."

My partner and I proceeded to the address and decided to drive through the alley first. We were rolling down the alley with the lights off but weren't sure which building it was. We headed to the front, found the address and parked the car. Our complainant could probably give us a little more background into the problems he was having so we went into the three-flat and rang his buzzer.

Sure enough, Mr. Mohammed appeared... all 98 pounds of him. He was a skinny little east-Indian dressed in pajamas. There wasn't much of a story behind this call so we decided to check the yard and see what we could find. Mr. Mohammed decided he would follow us and wait at the mouth of the gangway. Assuring him that we would check things out, my partner and I proceeded to the rear of the building with one hand shining our flashlights and one hand on our guns. Mr. Mohammed watched, wide eyed.

The gangway was narrow and completely dark, not even enough room for us to walk side by side. Just as we were about to reach the backyard, our good sergeant pulled into the alley behind the building. He would cover the rear, and also write us down on his log. Just one problem with this. His squad car scared a skunk that was out for a midnight stroll. The skunk shot right up the gangway, right at us. Retreat was our only option.

With a quick yell, my partner and I were running at full speed, right towards our complainant. Our keys were slapping together, nightsticks clanking against our radios, and the beams from our flashlights were going from ground to sky with every stride. Mr. Mohammed could also run fast. It must have been a half a block before we caught up to him and assured him we were only running from a skunk. He never blinked his eyes or said a word to us as we explained that there was no one in his yard. I still laugh thinking about what he saw. Two of Chicago's finest, twice his size, running right for him with fear in their eyes. It probably took him awhile to calm down and get back to sleep.

He hasn't called us back since that night.

All I Ever Had (Fiction)

By Rick Tippins

Today was a normal day on the job, if you can call any day on the job in the LAPD a normal day. I guess if someone didn't die or someone wasn't raped, that might constitute an abnormal day. God damn the sun is bright today, thank God for Oakley. I slide my wraparound sunglasses on and head to my patrol car. I've been a cop fifteen years, and although I could do this pre shift inspection in my sleep, I can't help running through the mental check list. Check the vehicle for damage, *don't want to find damage four hours into my shift and have to take the rap for an accident I wasn't even in.* Is the car gassed, are the guns loaded and ready to go, is the trunk full of all the gear I could ever need for any type call? Hell, some of this gear is designed for calls the crooks

haven't even come up with yet.

I love my job, well, maybe I tolerate my job.

Actually when I think about it, really honestly think

about it, it's not the job that irritates me, it's the

people. All the whining civilians we get paid to spoon

feed day in and day out, and the cops, my God the

cops are the worst. I grimace as I think about the

source of pretty much all my aggravation...humans.

The car checks out and I start it, turning the AC

on, waiting for my partner Frank. I can picture him in

the Sergeant's office with his lips fastened to our

boss's rear end tighter than one of those high-end

breast milk pumps. I dated a girl a few years back,

who had a three month old baby, and she had one of

those units. She'd hook up like a Holstein and pump

away. Sometimes she'd cook while she was pumping.

I mean no joke, walk around the kitchen cooking with

this contraption hanging off the front of her. Two things about those machines, they're loud and expensive. It's not like the dairy industry hasn't had years to perfect those things, why so damn loud? I don't get it.

Ah, finally the car starts to feel cooler, as Frank walks out of headquarters and heads toward the car. Frank has been on the job for about eight years and is married with three kids. I don't know how many boys or girls he has, even though he talks about them nonstop. Guess I should pay attention in case there's ever a test.

I think about my daughter and a deep sadness laced feeling of shame washes over me. I talked to her mother by phone exactly three times before we met for dinner. Two hours later we were a writhing, sweating, jumble of flesh. I always imagined us looking like two giant, wrestling anacondas, with our sweat slicked flesh glistening in the low light of a bathroom light I had purposely left on so I could get a good look at what I was getting into.

Although the wrestling match was noteworthy, I didn't feel compelled to ask for a re-match. I attributed the moment's perceived noteworthiness to the four vodkas I downed prior to, and during, dinner. The following morning I looked at Monica and quite simply put, was not moved. I never told her where I worked and only gave her my first name and cell phone number.

Two months later came the call every bachelor has nightmares about. She was keeping it and wanted to meet to talk things out. I agreed to meet her the next day at a coffee shop. On the following day I never went to the coffee shop and I changed my cell phone number. I haven't looked back and I hate when Frank talks about his kids. Monica tried to ruin my life and it is the most unsettling thing I can think about. Monica should have been a little more responsible or open to solutions other than child birth. I have a seven year old daughter...well not really, Monica has a daughter and she is probably married and the kid thinks the husband is her real dad...Life goes on and so do I.

I lean towards the air conditioning vent, welcoming the cold air as it washes over my face. I drink in its coolness, it helps clear my head. I find it weird how the coolness of an air conditioning vent, as processed as it is, feels so good. It's one of the few things I think feels better, than the real thing. Maybe it's because when you're being blasted by Mother Nature's version, you're usually freezing your backside off and aren't really in the mood for cold, I don't know.

I watch as Frank passes two other officers and I can just make out what they are saying, "Yo Frankie, Tommy ain't gonna wait all day while you kiss the Sergeant's butt." One officer slaps Frank on the back as he passes; Frank smiles and continues towards me. It's a smile, but it's not a smile. When people smile and I mean really smile, they put some effort into it. It's what I call the human glee pose. They hold it for a moment like a model striking her favorite pose. Her money maker if you will. The person smiling wants folks to know how they are feeling and that smile is gold. Frank's smile was not gold, he formed a smile, but instead of holding the pose, it vanished as soon as he turned from the two officers. His lips never parted and his teeth never showed. Frank hadn't smiled in the true sense.

Screw him, what did he expect? The guy started off in patrol then begged to go to the school resource unit. Who asks to go to a sissy unit like that? Guys like me get sent to those units as punishment. Frank reaches the car and gets in fully expecting a break from the brow beating. *I hate to disappoint you Frankie boy.* I look at him and just shake my head. This is by far the worst thing I can do to this guy. "What? I had to talk to him about some community policing stuff," Frank protests. I don't even look at him as I wheel the patrol car out of the parking lot and onto the road. *What did I ever do to deserve a partner like this guy?*

*****

Later in the shift, I've had probably a cup and a half too much coffee and am feeling a little jittery when the call comes out. The dispatcher's voice crackles over the radio, sweet as southern peach cobbler. I had another one of my "attention deficit disorder" moments and thought about all the female dispatcher's voices I've heard over my career. On a scale of 1-100, I would say 98 percent of them sounded super-hot on the radio, then I would meet them, thinking I was going to score and wow they were big and friendly and not my type. So I learned early on that our human senses are not always in sync with each other. While my ears were telling me 98 percent, my eyes were a little closer to 15 percent. I always go with my eyes, except on the rare occasion my nose steps in. The old adage "the nose knows" is absolutely true.

I physically feel Frank stiffen next to me and immediately do a rewind in my mind. I heard the radio traffic; I just wasn't paying attention, because I had been thinking about over weight police dispatchers. I look at the computer and read some of the details and catch the address and the crime. *A silent robbery alarm two blocks from us, we're probably going to contact this guy.* I reach down and switch on the lights, but leave the siren off as I start threading my way through the heavy traffic. A block from the scene, I see the suspect running on the sidewalk. I know he's the suspect, cops just know. I had a description plus who runs anywhere on hot day like today.

The suspect looks directly at me and I can see his eyes. I watch as those eyes go from a look of determination to panic, like a netted caribou. He turns and runs; I follow, still in the patrol car with Frank sitting next to me. I careen down the road passing dangerously close to pedestrians and other vehicles. I have a fast hard belief that if a bad guy wants to run down a sidewalk, I am content to drive down the street next to him. Let Bad Guy wear himself out, and when he decides to start jumping fences and engage in all that ridiculousness, I can hop out, fresh as tulips, and pursue an exhausted fugitive. Works like a charm, most of the time.

This is exactly how Homeboy decided to play it. I stayed in the car and marveled at the athleticism of this crook as he glided down the side walk at about a 4.4 second forty yard dash pace. It was like watching an NFL wide out flee the law...I had another moment and thought, *I wonder how many NFL players have run from the police since...1972.* Okay back on task, Homey was starting to get that look about him; he would be entering the yards soon in an attempt to break contact. "Get out here," I yelled to Frank. I slam on the brakes and Frank jettisons from the car. I speed up planning to pass Mr. Bad Guy so we can box him in. Bad guy keeps running, I can't figure out why he would do this, but I know one thing...He is separating me from Frank. *This isn't good; I will need*

Frank for the fight that seems to always accompany

any type of criminal pursuit.

The suspect rounds a corner and cuts through a parking lot and I can no longer see Frank. I don't know if he has fallen behind, lost us or what. Mr. Bad Guy turns sharply and leaps over a fence. *Time to sweat, Tommy boy.* I bail out of the car and clamber over the fence, and fall to the ground on the opposite side. I can see him; he's leaping over a second fence about fifteen yards away. The suspect gracefully negotiates several more fences as I follow in a far less graceful manner. It is an ugly game of celebrity follow the leader. I am playing the part of Shrek while the nimble Bad Guy is playing Baryshnikov. By the fourth fence, my hands are a little beat up. I grab the top heaving myself up and over, landing on my butt.

I feel sick, *whose legs are those? I'm gonna puke.* What just happened? I need to draw my gun, I need to get that done and get it done now. I glance down and my Glock is in its holster. Why isn't it in my hand? *Oh my God, I'm going to be sick.* For a split second, time and space allow me a full spectrum look at my situation. The suspect is winding up for a third strike and I don't think I can get out of the way. I've been struck twice already, once in the right arm...which I can't feel and once across the right collar bone. BAM! There's that third blow and I was right, I couldn't get out of the way. I roll on my side as the fourth shot strikes my Glock, breaking the handgrip and tearing it half way out of my holster. I can see the suspect's weapon, a four foot length of steel pipe. The last shot didn't do any real damage; I think I might be able to work this out long enough for Frank to get here.

The fifth blow glances off the back of my head and buries its self into my already damaged collar bone. *I don't want to die!* I'm crawling away, full retreat mode as the sixth blow lands squarely on my back, knocking most of the wind out of my heaving lungs. I roll on my back and stare up at the monster. He's black, dressed in clean clothes, looks scared and the guy isn't even sweating. He looms over me for a brief moment, eying me like a predator who has outmatched its prey, confusion has set in. He was expecting better of me, and I disappointed him. Maybe he'd been at odds with officers in the past that'd showed more bravado than I was showing.

I might be okay here, "You can go man." He ignores my offer, hefting the pipe for a seventh blow. "Don't do this man, you're killing me." *I can't die, I'll beg if I have to.* "I'll pay you man, anything you want, take my gun, take all my gear man," I claw at my gun belt, but can't get it off. The Velcro that has always served to keep my bat belt secure around my waist is stopping me from tossing it, and all its wonderful tools, on the bargaining table.

The seventh blow hits hard and was the worse thus far. It struck across my right knee and I scream in a chaotic blend of pain and panic, more of the later at this point. "I have a family, a seven year old daughter for Christ Sake man." As the words pour out of my mouth, shame washes over me like a tsunami. I was asking for help from my seven year daughter who I had never seen and worse yet, never tried to see. I wondered if she had ever cried out for an absent father who had never been there and would never come. I cried out, I didn't know her name so I just scream, "Baby, baby, don't let me die here." The tears are streaming down my face and I am overcome by waves of self-pity. "Dear God man let me go home to my daughter." BAM! The eighth blow lands across my cheek bone. "I'll do anything, stop...please, don't hit me again."

The shot to my cheek really hurt me and I am not talking about ouch, that hurt, get me a Band-Aid type pain. The eighth shot to my face launched my boat. I am drifting down a river and my mind is all over the place, *dispatchers...those big, big dispatchers, why? I suspect it's because they sit all day, and eat. What else is there to do in that cave they call a dispatch center? Why does artificially cooled air feel so good and artificially sweetened food can't hold a candle to the real thing?*

Frank has three kids, two boys and a girl, I remember now. BAM! Number nine hits somewhere on the back of my shoulders. *I'm gonna take a little nap and when I wake up Mr. Bad Guy is going to be gone.* I start a lazy drift down a stream. I wonder why they call them dead beat dads. *I'm about to be a beat dead dad, can a person be both, well I'm about to find*

out.

*****

A week later I wake in the hospital, bandages wrapped around every part of my body. I find a cast on my right arm and I can't see too well. *God my head hurts...ah for Christ sakes, my whole being hurts. Where the heck am I?* I look around and see all the staples of a hospital room. The memories flood back, the suspect, the pipe, the blows, the pain, and the drifting away. My mouth is so dry it feels like I slept with the business end of a blow dryer stuffed in it. My God there is a bag of urine hanging on the bed next to me. From the urine bag, tubes are routed up the side of the bed and disappear beneath the blanket...near my crouch! *At least I was out for that.*

A day later, Frank walks into my hospital room. The memories flood my brain, the begging, the pleading, the use of my abandoned daughter in an effort to save my own miserable life.

"How you feeling?" I just stare at Frank for a long moment.

"Where were you?" I ask. "I was there Tommy, I killed the guy. I just had a hell of a time getting over that last fence."

I stare at Frank and ponder shaking my head, but decide against it, mostly because it would hurt too much to do so.

"I saw most of what he did to you," Frank says somberly.

I turn my head away, if he saw most of what happened to me, he heard everything. Frank heard me beg for my life and stoop below low and use my daughter, whose name I didn't even know. I stare out the window for a while longer... "Please leave."

Frank turns, hesitates and looks back. "I didn't know you had a daughter."

I tighten my jaw, staring at nothing. "Go."

Seven weeks later both Frank and I are decorated for bravery. Mr. Bad Guy had been responsible for over twenty robberies and seven murders, two of which were women. I limped off the stage and went straight to the bar where I drank myself into a phlegmatic state of unfeeling. I stayed that way for four months until I found out I was being retired from the force due to my injuries. Life went from bad to worse in the matter of one foot pursuit.

*****

I'm sitting in my apartment, my loaded service weapon is lying next to me and ESPN is on the television. More NFL players arrested, *why aren't NHL players arrested? I'll have to look into that later.* I just got forcibly retired, and if I hadn't, I'm not sure I could have gone back after being so thoroughly beaten down by Mr. Bad Guy. My daughter flashes across my mind, and the shame flushes through my system like an evil transfusion. I flex in a partial attempt to gain my feet. I'm going to Monica's house to make things right. I slump back into the couch and exhale until my lungs are empty and I feel light headed. I don't even know where she lives.

For the first time in my life, I see who I really am. I'm a weak man who has spent over a decade in law enforcement using smoke and mirrors to make myself appear strong. Yeah I would jump into a fight first, but only if there were several cops right behind me. All the great things I'd ever done as a cop were done with a safety net. I'd never stood alone and faced adversity, including being a father to a little girl.

I was fifty percent responsible for the birth of a human being and I refused to accept that responsibility. I abandoned a child, my child. The service weapon feels good in my hand and it feels natural to curl the weapon into my mouth... no not the mouth the temple. If I haven't been a man, was I ever really a cop? I called out to a seven year old girl when I was dying and expected help after I had abandoned her. Neither of those were the actions of a man or cop. It's a hard thing to look into the mirror expecting to see one thing and see something else, ugly, weak and undesirable and realize that thing is you.

One of the many questions associated with life is clear to me now. Life is like a clock, it has a starting point and an ending point. No matter the path one's life takes, there is always a beginning and an ending. My second hand was fast approaching the twelve where it would join its friends, hour and minute hands.

Wow, I can feel the grind of the trigger as I apply pressure, transforming the weapon from a static piece of iron to a lethal entity. I need to end it all, the pain, the false identity, my shame. The thought that I am not even drunk makes the situation seem almost comical. *Don't all cops kill themselves after they have been drinking?* It seemed like something I'd heard, but I couldn't be certain. Maybe I should get a drink, and then finish this. Without warning the hammer drops.

Frank stands ready to knock on my front door along with Monica and a young girl. The firing pin strikes the primer and ignites the gun powder. I'm at peace for the first time as the propellant burns, turning from solid form to a gaseous substance, building pressure within the casing. My daughter, I would have named her Tara, she would have been beautiful...she is beautiful. The world and Tara will be better without me. I can taste metal, the end is near, or maybe it's over and I just don't know it. As the hot piece of copper-jacketed lead begins its journey through my skull, I see life as it should have been. *Tara, I love you. You're really all I've ever had.*

On the Fence

By Jay Padar

As I hung there upside down from the six-foot chain link fence I knew I was in trouble. It was dark and secluded. We were the only two people in sight. He saw my vulnerability and knew that this was his chance to exploit it. The smirk on his face let me know that I needed to act immediately. Calling for backup was not an option. As he walked slowly towards me I saw his hand start to reach. I put my hand on my gun, unsnapped it and slid it out of my holster. With a string of expletives I advised him in no uncertain terms that I would not be his victim tonight. The tone in my voice and fire in my eyes let him know that if he followed through with his plan, it would come at a price; a price he might not be willing to pay.

My partner and I were a couple hours into our midnight shift when we got the call. He wasn't my regular partner but we worked well together and trusted each other. It was a routine burglar alarm at a commercial business.

"Generic burglar alarm, key holder notified and will be on scene in about 30 minutes" said our dispatcher.

We crept down the block slowly with our lights off and parked a couple doors down. We exited the squad car and quietly pushed the doors shut as to not alarm any potential intruders of our arrival. With our radios turned down and flashlights in hand we approached the front and scanned the front and side windows and door. All appeared to be secure. As we walked to the back we came to a six foot chain link fence separating us from the rear door and windows.

Our view of the building was now obstructed by the crates and dumpsters.

He was the first to go over the fence as I covered him. I followed after his safe landing. With our hands on our guns we checked the rear door and windows. All secure. I notified our dispatcher to give any other responding units a disregard. As I turned back to the fence I noticed that my partner had already made it over and was heading back towards our car. I scaled the fence, put one foot on top and attempted to push myself over. As I did my shoelaces on my right boot got tangled on the fence. I came crashing down, head just inches from the pavement, swinging upside down. Try as I might, I couldn't reach the laces with my knife. I hung there upside down and took a deep breath contemplating my next move.

That's when he approached. I heard his footsteps and then saw him slowly emerge from the shadows. The grin on his face was ear to ear. His laugh was devious. As he began to reach I started my tirade and drew my weapon. He paused for a moment but called my bluff. With a hearty laugh he grabbed the mic and called out.

"Squad, does anyone on the zone have a camera?"

Yes, prior to the days of camera phones, my partner was trying to capture this priceless moment on film before I could get myself down. My language and threats of retaliation got stronger. Before the dispatcher could respond my partner keyed the mic again and gave a disregard.

I breathed a sigh of relief and muttered, "Cut me down, asshole."

With a smile and a laugh he cut my laces as I did a handstand to keep myself from landing on my head. Back on my feet we walked back to our squad parked in front.

"That could have been so bad," I said.

"It could have been so good," he answered.

A Woman in a Man's World: Living inside a Correctional Institution.

By Harriet Fox

When I was growing up, I wanted to be a dentist. And a brain surgeon. And a racecar driver. Never once did I say I wanted to be a Correctional Officer. No one ever says, "I am going to be a Correctional Officer when I grow up." Some days I wonder how in the world I ended up at a job locked up in county jail twelve hours a day.

Wasn't I going to have a cool desk job where you wear high heels and carry a briefcase to the high rise office building and sit at a desk overlooking the amazing city?

I'm in a high rise building alright. Just instead of a view, I am watching inmates. Instead of high heels, I am wearing combat boots. Instead of a briefcase, I'm carrying a tactical backpack.

So, how did I end up behind bars with the evil individuals of society? There's a running joke amongst my peers that we as correctional officers have a life sentence just like some criminals do. Being a correctional officer is the most thankless job. It's a very negative, abusive, monotonous, dank environment where you may be hated for the uniform you wear. You are no longer seen as a person, but instead as an authority figure, a rival, the enemy.

We look at the bad guys as evil. And they look at us as evil. It's always a cat and mouse game with criminals. And almost twelve years later, I have a love/hate relationship with my job.

Being a female in Corrections definitely requires a tough skin, a sense of humor, and patience. This job has taught me how to be a better enforcer, an authority figure, a parent, a mentor or counselor, a professional babysitter, and a disciplinarian. Being a correctional officer consists of wearing many hats. And you may be called upon to switch those hats many times in one shift.

I knew early on I wanted to work in law enforcement. I grew up running through the halls of my father's police department. I remember how I always looked up to my father and his police partners who were protecting the city and dealing with the bad guys. I have always had a desire to do the right thing and make sure the bad guys could no longer hurt innocent people in society.

My folks and I watched a lot of cop movies as I was growing up. Cop shoot 'em up movies. In the movies, I learned the cops always won in the end, but the message of those movies left an everlasting mark on my mind that bad guys hurt people. Innocent people.

I learned early on my desire to keep people safe, as well as that I wanted to be righteous. Something formed inside me that I wanted to always do the right thing and to be as good as I could be so I would be the farthest away from the wrong, the evil, and the criminals.

I thought I would have become a cop. When I was in college studying Criminal Justice, I lived and breathed the work it would take to become a police officer. I worked for two police departments and volunteered at my father's department. In the process of my law enforcement career, as years passed by, I stumbled across the local Sheriff's Department where I did not leave after becoming a correctional officer. Ever since my arrival, I am a woman in a man's world.

When I applied for the corrections job, I remember showing up to find myself among what seemed like hundreds to take the written test. We all file into a room and sit down. I look over to see football player looking guys ripped with large muscles and twice the height of me. I sat there thinking to myself, *how can I compete with these guys?* Needless to say, I passed the written test, interviews, polygraph, medical and psychological screenings. And was hired with none of those muscular guys.

This taught me I can just be me.

Have I been seen as a female and not as an equal? At times. Have people told me women do not belong in this line of work? Sure. But I know that my actions and the job I do have never wavered. I have somehow proven I am fit for the job, both mentally and physically. Females can do the job just as well as males. Women's strategies or their presentations of self may be different, but the job can be done successfully all the same. I never felt the need to compete with a man; I just do what I have to do.

I have never denied my limitations and quickly learned to use my strengths and weaknesses to my advantage. It turned out my weaknesses were not really weaknesses after all.

I am not saying all women belong in law enforcement. I am not saying I have not been discriminated against. I am not saying I did not have to work twice as hard to prove myself to my coworkers or to the inmates. I am not saying I am as physically strong as the male correctional officers I work with. But I can say that in the decade plus of years on the job, I have never let my coworkers down.

Since the day I started this job, it was my purpose to be the best correctional officer I could be and to always have my partners' backs. Recognizing my limitations did not mean I felt inferior or was at a loss of confidence. It just meant I learned my job and found what worked best for me, whether it was learning better verbal skills to engage inmates, what worked to diffuse volatile situations, or learning how I could maintain order on a housing unit. I never fought the role of being a female.

During my first jail shift, assigned to my first Jail Training Officer, he received the assignment of writing a crime report for an assault on another deputy. This deputy had been employed for years and was spat in his eye after an altercation with an inmate.

I remember looking at the male deputy who appeared strong and competent and thought, *what did I just get myself into?!*

But I plugged on, passed training, and here I am today.

When I arrive at work, I show up as a correctional officer, not a petite 5'1" female. I wear nail polish and mascara and I have long hair that I wear pinned up in a bun. I come to work to do my job, and to do it well. I can say I learn something new every day. I have worked extremely hard to be accepted by my male counterparts and strive every day to uphold the job I swore to do.

The common perception in society is that women are generally weaker and less assertive than men. Those who believe this allow these stereotypes to travel into the workplace.

Corrections is not like we see on television or in the movies. There are no bars in newer jail facilities, the keys are not archaic, and there is nothing sexy about a pair of handcuffs in my world. My handcuffs have been on the wrists of murderers, child molesters, rapists, drug addicts, and psychopaths. This job is far from normal but to those of us who do it, it is normal.

It is not every day people go to work to get called every name in the book, assaulted, or tried to be manipulated.

Every day we lace up our boots knowing we may be risking our lives that shift. The mindset is no matter what, we go home at the end of shift.

I have been involved in hundreds of altercations over the years. And if I break a nail, I still get pissed off to this day.

Anyone who works this job knows assaults are imminent and confrontation with hostile inmates will happen. It's all in how a correctional officer handles themselves when faced with these situations. I cannot say I have always had the outcomes to these situations as I had hoped, but overall, my injuries have been extremely minimal and I have learned from any mistake along the way. I may not have encountered every situation yet.

But I'm saying I've held my own.

I have worked a housing unit alone. I have worked the Administrative Segregation Unit, more commonly known as the maximum security unit. I have dealt with the violently mentally ill, gang members, murderers, and cop killers. I have never been preyed on by inmates or would ever cross any integrity lines towards corruption.

I am one of very few females who have become a member of the Emergency Response Team. I know I'm a valued and productive member of my team.

We are a group of ten members who are committed to resolving critical incidents within our correctional facilities as well as using tactics that emphasize control, containment, and resolution with the goal of protecting life and property. Basically we are SWAT inside the jail walls. We use specialized equipment and wear tactical padding.

I have to admit, being the only girl on my Emergency Response Team, I love being a part of the good ol' boys club. We go in and handle business. To be a girl who gets to suit up in a bunch of gear equivalent to a football player, it is like playing house. But better. I get such a rush. I am honored my male teammates trust me. I do what I signed up for.

First time we had to extract two inmates from one cell, we briefed before responding to the housing unit.

The two inmates were in jail for serious charges: one for attempted murder on a cop and the other for murder of a gang member. Both were gang members who were still active in their gang.

The window of their cell was covered so we could not get a visual. This can be dangerous entering a cell when you have no cooperation and it is unknown if there are weapons inside. It is unknown if the inmate has intentions to hurt staff.

After negotiations, these guys were not backing down. We were going in.

Let me explain, I work for an agency that is a tad bit behind in the times. We do not have all the tools other jails have. We are plain old fashioned. We go in. In my opinion, I am not sure it is the best idea for staff's safety but we go in and do what we have to do to get inmates out and to a safer place.

So we make entry and the fight is on. We separate the line, three of us go to the back to gain control of the first inmate and a co-worker and I deal with the closer to the door. And instantly the fight is on. Minutes later, he is still fighting. He is punching my partner in the head. He is attempting to reach me too. At some point he looks at me and yells, "I give up! I can't hit a girl!" I am wearing a helmet and a balaclava. He recognizes me by my eyes. And the fight is over.

Sometimes I have seen things that just make me shake my head. We regularly say to each other how in disbelief we are over something we have seen or heard.

Through all these years, I have continued to strive, better myself, and learn as much as I can. I feel I have excelled at my written and verbal communication skills since this job relies on this. I am a skilled typist and write detailed reports. I have an inquisitive mind and allow it to run wild during my investigations. I have learned to communicate and work with hostile inmates, which has taught me patience. I have had to make quick decisions in emergency situations teaching me sound decision making.

I have worked on public speaking while assigned to a housing unit with up to 96 inmates conducting daily duties or pod meetings. I take pride in my integrity, work ethic, professionalism, and production of high quality work.

I am not afraid to ask for help and have had the opportunity to learn every job position within our two correctional facilities. I enjoy camaraderie and being a part of making a healthy work environment. Not a day goes by that I do not learn something new.

I am grateful for the training officers who taught me well. I am grateful for the co-workers and supervisors who guided me and helped me along the way. It is they who helped mold me into who I am today. I am grateful to my coworkers who believe in me as much as they do with the tall buff males I work alongside with. I know I have had no breaks and have been expected to compete and complete everything the same as my male counterparts.

I am grateful to my coworkers for accepting me as I am. Who they see is who I am: a person with common sense, a person with a good work ethic, and someone who has a willingness to be one of the guys.

So on my days off, I may be my alter ego wearing my hair down or throwing on a pair of heels from time to time. But I am probably most comfortable in my uniform and combat boots doing what comes natural to me.

My work is about being tough when I need to be and being a dedicated, loyal, team player all the time.

I'm living proof that working hard, being in this line of work for the right reasons, and loving the job molds an excellent correctional officer regardless of gender.

I have seen a lot in my years as a correctional officer. There is no question that I will continue to see more over the years until I retire. I will no doubt see more unleashed chaos, inmate manipulation, assaults, and pure evil.

I did not become a police officer like I envisioned but I am still doing what I set out to do many years ago. As I sit at my work station in the middle of the night, while the rest of the word sleeps, one thing I know is I am keeping society safe from evil. I am making sure the bad guys no longer hurt innocent people during my watch.

Shootout at the High Rollers Pool Hall:

Prelude to a Family Tragedy.

By Jim Padar

(Communications tapes

www.OnBeingaCop.com/soundtracks/shootout.mp3**)**

It was 1974, on a cold February afternoon in Chicago, as I headed for the 4:30 roll call at Maxwell Street, Area Four Detective Headquarters. I would be late. I had tarried too long with my wife at the nearby hospital where she had been admitted to be prepped for an operation the following day. A persistent, suspicious lump on Karla's left breast would be examined surgically. She was characteristically upbeat as always and I found it difficult to tear myself away, but I finally made the break. I would return early tomorrow to see her off to the operating room.

The red brick building at Maxwell and Morgan was built in 1889 and was a classic old Chicago Police Station.

The single long flight of marble steps leading to the second floor detective squad room had paths worn an inch or two deep at each side rail where cops with bad guys in tow had trudged over the previous 85 years. It would become known to a nation of television fans as the "Hill Street Blues" precinct because this is where the opening scenes of the popular 1980's show were filmed. To those of us who worked the murders it was just Maxwell Street Homicide.

I would be with my steady partner Mike Shull. Mike and I worked together with comfort and confidence that had developed after spending many months together, cruising the west side in search of the killer du jour. And as a bonus he had an offbeat, intellectual sense of humor that made our hours together pass quickly.

"Padar, Shull, you've got 13," announced the sergeant as he read the assignment sheet. That meant our radio call for evening would be 7413. Seven designated the Detective Division, four was Area Four, and thirteen would be our homicide car for the eight-hour tour. It wouldn't be the last time that the number 13 figured in events of the night.

As was customary, incoming cases would be rotated among all the homicide units working that night. Since my wife was scheduled for surgery early the following morning, I wanted to be sure to visit with her before they took her to the OR. We asked the sergeant for the first assignment of the night so as to lessen the chance of getting stuck with a late job. He obliged us a little over an hour later with a shooting victim at the Cook County Hospital. We interviewed the victim of a minor gunshot wound along with two witnesses, put out an all-call for the offender and stopped by a few locations he was known to frequent. Being a chilly February night it was highly unlikely that we would draw another assignment. Our chances of having to work overtime were now very slim.

As the tour of duty drew to a close, a forecast "light snow" started to dust the drab west side landscape. Mike and I decided to make one last semi-circle of the Area and then head into the office for the 12:30 AM check-off roll call. I'd be home and in bed by 1 AM, grab a few hours sleep and head out to the hospital. It was shortly after midnight, the radio was dead quiet and the streets were deserted as we coasted to a stop at the westbound traffic light at Madison and Homan. A man ran down the center of the street and when his feet hit the ground there was a momentary puff of the new fallen snow. He left a trail of giant footprints running straight toward our car. As a long time ghetto resident, he could spot an unmarked squad at a hundred yards.

Mike glanced at me as Mr. Citizen approached our car; "This guy done jus' got robbed." said Mike.

I rolled down my driver's window. It was exactly 13 minutes past midnight. In police time, 0013 hours.

"In da pool hall! Dey dere right now stickin' up everybody!"

"How many are there?" I asked.

"Dey's like fo' of em. An' dey got guns!"

"Okay, okay we got it." I replied as I picked up the mic from the dashboard. "Seventy-four-thirteen emergency."

"Go ahead seven-four-one three," replied the City Wide 2 dispatcher instantly.

"Yeah, there's a robbery-in-progress..." I glanced across Homan to the south side of the street through the snow. No chance of getting an address. A...at Madison and Homan, in the pool hall."

I killed the headlights and pulled our car slowly across Homan to the north curb of Madison directly across from the pool hall.

"Madison and Homan in the pool hall, a robbery-in-progress," barked the dispatcher.

A moment before Mike and I could have believed we were the only police unit on the streets of Chicago's west side but the quiet radio jumped to life as the Task Force and

Canine Units on our frequency responded in a flurry of overlapping jumbled transmissions, sirens screaming in the background. There was lots of help out there!

City-wide dispatch took the air again, "All right, quite a few units pretty close to that, they're comin' there, so units be careful now, that's a robbery-in-progress called in by seven-four-one- three, that's a homicide car. Madison and Homan in the pool hall."

Those were the last words we heard as we got out of the car, leaving our communications firmly affixed to control head mounted under the dashboard. In 1974 the department was in the final stages of transitioning from car-mounted radios to personal radios that would clip to your equipment belt. The Detective Division was last on the list for the new radios. In the parlance of the day, we were Aleaving the air."

As we left the squad, we looked across the street at the "High Roller's #4 Pool Hall." The plate glass windows were completely fogged with condensation. It would be best to stay on the north side of the street and use the squad for at least partial cover. Mike and I drew our 2" barrel, five shot, snub nose revolvers and rested our arms on the roof of the car as we peered intently through the light snow at the doorway of the pool hall. A total of ten rounds of ammo against four armed robbers seemed to put us at a decided disadvantage. By now our city-wide dispatcher had notified the district dispatcher and in the distance we heard the distinctive wail of city-wide and district units approaching. Good ol' Area Four! But for a few seconds the scene was almost idyllic; the red neon of the pool hall reflecting on the undisturbed snow softly falling on a deserted tranquil street. It would have made a great urban streetscape painting that you might find in an upscale gallery on North Michigan Avenue.

We didn't have long to wait before all that changed. Four robbers with dark clothing strangely punctuated with red ski masks burst through the door onto the sidewalk, broad shouldering each other as they competed for space in their haste to exit.

"Halt, police!" We yelled to the very much-surprised group. They paused in a moment of indecision. One of them raised a weapon, and fired a shot in our direction. It went wild into the park behind Mike and me. They too heard the sirens in the distance and while I have no way of knowing if it figured into their decision, they turned east and as a group fled southeast through the parking lot next to the pool hall. Using the squad roof to steady our arms and with a firm two handed grip, Mike and I squeezed off several rounds. The department's regulation high pressure ammunition was designed for four inch barrel revolvers and as a result each round squeezed out of the two inch snub-nose seemed to envelop my hands in a burst of flame and unburnt powder as it spewed from the cylinder and barrel. One, two, three rounds I counted and 16-year-old

Tyree Brewston hit the ground as if a Bears fullback had hit him. In reality it was only a 38 Special +P Hollow Point entering his left buttock and exiting his scrotum. Tyree wasn't going any further tonight but his older companions fled south on Homan never looking back. I made a mental note that I had only two rounds left if should they return for their wounded companion. In retrospect it was a ludicrous thought... attempting to imply a Marine mentality to a rag-tag group of ghetto robbers. I fingered the bullet pouch on my belt for a split second but the approaching sirens convinced me that a reload would not be necessary.

The first assist unit was now pulling up, westbound on Madison. They stopped between the parking lot and us. Fate ruled that they just happened to be a canine unit. With a light snow falling, and two dogs, pursuit shouldn't be a trick.

"Shots fired, shots fired!" I shouted to them. "We've got one down in the parking lot." I was hoping that they would relay the information to dispatch. Our radio was firmly attached inside our locked vehicle. Unfortunately that did not happen. With a fluid situation that was still developing, the initial units arriving elected to take care of business on the street and pursue the escaping robbers. The result was several minutes of confusion for the poor dispatchers. The second assist unit was a district beat car and they cautiously approached Tyree who lay writhing in the snow. They collared a passing wagon for transport to the hospital. Mike and I headed into the pool hall. We had just shot a guy. The next order of business was to corral victims and witnesses and phone our boss!

Time swirled around us. The scene was almost surreal but neither Mike nor I would recall any excitement or panic. Behind the scenes our citywide dispatcher had notified the district zone dispatcher of the robbery-in-progress, still unaware that shots had been fired. Additional 11th District beat cars were enroute from all directions. The wagon loaded up Tyree and headed to Mount Sinai Hospital. As more beat cars arrived with lights and sirens the street was literally wall-to-wall squad cars parked askew, mars lights still flashing. The previous scene of a lone unmarked homicide car pulling quietly to the curb had been transformed in a matter of a few moments to one worthy of the ten o'clock news. Given the hour however the news crews were thankfully tucked in for the night. We started to gather vital information, victims, witnesses, and addresses. Canine and Task Force reported apprehending two additional offenders. It was becoming apparent that several of our robbery victims and witnesses had disappeared in the confusion. Our concern was very real... we had just shot a man and our cast of eyewitnesses was slipping away. We heard some talk that the canine unit had also recovered a weapon. In the pool hall Mike grabbed a personal radio from a district officer.

"Seventy-four-thirteen on the Zone..." Mike called.

"Seventy-four thirteen go ahead," responded the District dispatcher.

"We're here at the scene of the robbery in the pool hall, and any beat cars that are out in this area workin' on this, would they bring the patrons back to this location for interview. Any of those beat cars that have any of those patrons and victims of the robbery would they please bring them back to the scene."

Out of a packed pool hall of multiple victims we would wind up with only six robbery complainants/witnesses. Weeks later, only one would show up in court to testify to the robbery.

It was a full 18 minutes before we were able to return to our radio and give a report to our City-Wide 2 dispatcher.

Outside once again in our squad I keyed the mike, "Seven-four-one-three, do we have the canine car that recovered that weapon from that robbery-in-progress? Please return to the scene here with that weapon."

"Yeah he is on the way to ya and also four-thirteen clarify... were there shots fired by the police?"

It was now almost 20 minutes into the incident and our citywide dispatcher and the district dispatcher had no details of the shooting. The ten year old "state of the art" communications center was located in the headquarters building just south of Chicago's loop. District zone dispatchers were housed on one floor and the city-wide dispatchers were on another floor and the detective units at the scene had radios, but they were firmly anchored to the dashboard of their vehicles. Such was the state of Chicago Police communications in the mid-seventies.

"Yes, there were shots fired by the police," I replied "...and there is one offender who is hit, he is on his way to Mount Sinai Hospital, his condition appears to be good at the present time."

"All right, is this by four-thirteen?"

"The shots were fired by four-thirteen, that is correct."

"All right, were there any shots fired back at the police?"

"Yes sir, there were shots fired at us," I said.

"All right that's what I had to find out here... ah four-thirteen... there's no police officers injured though?"

"Negative, no police officers injured."

There was a flurry of questions, who was going where, command personnel who were responding and then there was a momentary break in radio traffic. An anonymous unit broke silence.

"Police one... offenders nothing."

Back at the Maxwell Street station there was all the fanfare that accompanies a police shooting; Commanders, Deputy Superintendents, Internal Affairs, States Attorneys, and a court reporter to take official statements from Mike and me. We would later recall that we probably experienced more stress during the next several hours than we did in those fateful few seconds on West Madison Street.

The "occasional snow" continued falling throughout the night. I glanced anxiously at my watch. It was after 5 AM and my wife's surgery was scheduled in less than three hours. I felt a need to go home before heading for the hospital and the snow would be a problem. After a few consultations the bosses agreed to let Mike complete the remaining paperwork and I was released from my tour of duty shortly after 5:30 AM.

The occasional snow now amounted to several inches but I hit the expressway before the rush hour and made it home while it was still dark. In the bathroom I scrubbed my hands vigorously and discovered tiny reddish black marks that burned under the soap and brush. I dashed cold water in my face and then I tiptoed into the boy's room and touched each one of them. Chris 5, Craig

3½, and Jay just 8 weeks old were sleeping soundly. I stroked their backs ever so gently. For the first time I felt some emotion as tears welled up. I brushed my eyes and was surprised at the faint smell of gunpowder residue that remained on my hands.

Karla's mother was taking care of the children... "Jim?" she called from the other bedroom. "Are you okay?"

I moved to the hallway before answering, "Yes," I whispered. "I had to work late—it's snowing pretty good. I'm heading out to the hospital."

At the hospital it was obvious that Karla had been crying. I sat down on her bed and gave her a hug and a kiss. I told her she looked scared, she told me I looked tired. There was a roommate the other side of the curtain between the two beds but I had no idea who it was.

"I had to work late," I replied. "You know they can give you something to relax you." They gave her a shot and we held hands.

She loved good-natured kidding, especially if it was at my expense but this morning nothing came. Neither of us was up to it. When they arrived to take her to surgery I walked her to the elevator doors holding her hand all the way. When the doors opened she kissed my hand and suddenly brightened.

"Your hands are dirty!" she said shaking her head in mock exasperation as the elevator doors slid shut between us.

As she headed to surgery Karla would be alone in a very real sense. There would be no partner at her side, no sirens in the distance heralding imminent rescue. Indeed for the next several months it would seem as though the entire medical profession would abandon her.

*****

It was just a year past that long day and I was speaking with Karla's oncologist late one afternoon. Things were not going well and she had been hospitalized for the past several days. The doctor spoke of a new experimental chemotherapy and we agreed to start treatment that very afternoon.

Early that evening I sat with her in room 1007A at Rush-Presbyterian-St. Luke's. She told me our pastor had visited but she was noncommittal about the details.

"We prayed." was all she would say and then suddenly, she looked at me with tears welling up in her eyes and asked, "When am I ever going to be okay?"

I encouraged her to give the new medicine a chance to take effect and as visiting hours drew to a close I kissed her good night.

Out in my car on VanBuren Street I slid in behind the wheel. With tears streaming down my face I gripped the wheel, closed my eyes and prayed aloud:

"Dear Lord, if you are going to take her, please... take her now."

There were tears but none of the heart pounding panic of the previous months...just a sense of peace and resignation. I sat quietly for a several minutes and dried my eyes and then I headed home on the Kennedy Expressway with a sense of fatigue but also of peace.

It is said that coincidence is God's way of remaining anonymous. As I hung my coat in the front closet the doorbell rang. It was my brother and sister. They had gone to visit at the hospital but had arrived too late for visiting hours. On a whim they decided to stop by and visit me. Almost simultaneously the phone rang. It was the hospital. Karla had taken a sudden turn for the worse, could I please return as quickly as possible?

My brother drove. My sister sat in the back seat crying quietly.

"Oh Jim, oh Jim," she repeated over and over.

As we headed back towards the city on the expressway I implored my brother not to speed or take chances. Deep inside I knew two things for certain; it was over and I would not be alone. My brother and sister were with me tonight and Karla's family would surround the boys and me with love and support in the coming months and years. Maybe God had a plan...

Encounter

By Jay Padar

Our encounter only lasted for a matter of seconds. It happened fourteen years ago, but I think about it more often than I'd like to. I think about it intently every year at Christmas time. My stare would have, I'm sure, made him feel uncomfortable or uneasy, but I'm certain he never knew I was there. If he saw the way I was staring at him he would have sensed my helplessness and fear. That intent stare had an adverse effect on me. It locked his image in my memory for an eternity I'm afraid. It's an image, I fear, that won't ever go away. That image is the reason I hold my three year old boy's hand a little too tight when crossing the street. It's the reason I carry my son's twin sister across the street when she tells me that she can walk on her own. It was an event that the police academy did not, could not prepare me for. My instructors made me faster and stronger. They made me smarter and more knowledgeable. However, there are experiences on the street that lectures and gym exercises just can't prepare you for. This was one of them.

The date was December 24th, 1998. I had graduated from the police academy just ten days prior and was about as green as a new police officer could be. My "veteran" partner for the night had been on the street for about a year and a half. Thinking back I laugh about how highly I regarded his experience. He was, and still is, a solid police officer, but at the time he was just a kid like me. We were working the afternoon shift on Christmas Eve just hoping to get off on time. Right before the end of our shift the dispatcher apologetically assigned us the call.

"Sorry 2444, but we have a pedestrian struck by a hit and run driver at Rockwell and Devon. There are no other cars available. Fire is on the way."

My partner hit the gas and proceeded to the scene. At first glance we were relieved. No pedestrian down, no ambulance and no commotion on the street. As we happily informed the dispatcher that we couldn't find any victim, she advised us that the victim was taken by cab to St. Francis Hospital. Alright, he can't be in bad shape if he took a cab to the hospital. We'll race there, knock out a quick report and be at check off on time. Our Christmas was just a few hours away.

We walked into the emergency room and let the receptionist know that we were there for the hit and run victim. Our cavalier demeanor changed dramatically when she informed us that he was in trauma room three... and his parents were with the chaplain in the private waiting area. I walked hurriedly into the ER and pulled the curtain back at trauma room three. That's when my eyes locked onto him. His naked and bloodied little body lay lifeless on the gurney. The doctors and nurses worked feverishly to revive him. They were pumping his chest and working on him in a manner I can only describe as controlled chaos. They were working on him the way a dying three year old boy deserved to be worked on. All of the medical technology available and intense effort by emergency room staff would not be enough to save this little boy. His short life would end tonight.

After what seemed like an eternity, I closed the curtain and walked slowly to the private waiting area. It is a waiting area where no one wants to be. His father sat sobbing in a chair with his head in his hands, clothes soaked with his little boy's blood. He had held his son in the cab on the way to the hospital. His mother sat almost expressionless, in a state of shock holding their newborn baby as the hospital chaplain spoke softly to her. I knew I could offer no comfort or be of any help to anyone. I could sense the uneasiness in my partner as he told me he had never handled a fatal accident before and that he was going to request that Major Accidents respond to the hospital. Even though, as the passenger in the patrol car, it was my job to handle the paperwork for this, my partner thankfully took the reins and completed what was necessary.

Detectives from the Major Accident Investigation Unit, who investigate all fatal traffic accidents, arrived shortly afterwards and began their investigation. They asked the hard questions like the boy's name and birthday, how did this happen and what did the car look like that hit him. It turns out that this young family was visiting from Indiana. They had just finished a late dinner at a restaurant when dad went out to warm up the car. Mom waited in the restaurant for a few minutes and then carried their newborn in her arms as their three year old held onto her finger while walking alongside her. When the little boy saw his dad warming up the car across the street he let go of his mother's finger and ran into the street towards him. That's when the silver sports utility vehicle struck him. The little boy was dragged underneath the SUV for about a block before his body came to rest on the cold pavement. Not wanting to wait for an ambulance, his father picked up his little body and raced him to the hospital in a cab. I found out months later that the driver of the SUV had fled to Mexico after the accident. He later returned and was arrested.

I didn't speak of this incident the next morning celebrating Christmas at my parent's house with my family. It would be the first of many events throughout my police career that I wouldn't speak of. Someday, God willing, years from now my kids will be grown and read this story. And they'll understand why daddy held their hands a little too tight at times, and why they were carried across the street when they thought they were too big to be carried. Hopefully they'll understand how precious they are to me and how hard I've worked to protect them. And maybe, years from now, if they see me staring off into space at a Christmas Eve party, while everyone else is laughing and enjoying the celebration, they'll know that it's just that time of year where daddy must remember December 24th, 1998 and the moments spent with that other little boy.

Forty-Three Minutes (Fiction)

By C.L.Swinney

Startled by a loud cry, I woke up and shook my head, trying to figure out if the sound was real or only another bad dream. It seemed to be coming from somewhere close by and although the voice wasn't familiar to me, it caused me to sit up quickly, crane my neck, and listen. Sadly, I knew it wasn't coming from the girls' room. I was glad they weren't in distress, but they also weren't with me. My two daughters had been taken away when my wife left. The thought of losing them forever caused me to glance at my firearm on the nightstand. Next to it, the LED lights glowing on the clock read 3:02 AM. Not hearing anything further, I sat completely still, listening to my own heartbeat thumping in my ears, and wincing at the pounding in the front of my head. I listened awhile longer and didn't hear anything, so I rolled my eyes, dismissing the cry as yet another nightmare.

Sleep continued to elude me as my mind spun out of control. I thought about how day after day I worked chasing folks who made poor decisions in life. It always bothered me that if I didn't keep a level head during those encounters, someone might kill me. I've seen it in their eyes. Some of them have even told me so. Cops don't think about such things during the moment, and I'm no exception, but when I'm safe in my own home trying to sleep, the images of their faces or the people they've killed or mutilated, creep into my soul... and I ache. I wish I could save everyone or at least bring wrongdoers to justice, but it's not possible, and I struggle with that daily.

Boredom forced me to track down the TV controller and start surfing the channels. The pending court date for my daughters' child custody case was eating me up inside. My thoughts drifted to how I was supposed to be a tough guy, but I recalled crying on duty. Others wearing a badge have done the same. Some of them took their pain out on their family or others. I thought about the ones who took their own lives. It wasn't easy to shrug off the thought of people killing themselves, but moments earlier, a fleeting thought had crossed my mind as I'd noticed my duty weapon on the nightstand. I glanced again at the gun. It was still there. Jesus, get a grip, man. You have two daughters to live for. I caught myself getting overrun with guilt and remorse as evil coursed in my veins in the form of Jack Daniels. Somehow those terrible thoughts slipped away when I stumbled upon a Seinfeld rerun. The madness of the show interrupted the battle of the voices in my head.

Immediately after a commercial came on, there was a pause in the cable feed. It was quiet for a few seconds. Suddenly, I heard a blood-curdling scream coming from the house next door. I sprang out of bed, threw on some shorts and flip-flops, and turned to run toward the scream.

Spinning around, I sprinted back into my room to grab my service weapon.

The screaming continued and got increasingly louder as I approached my neighbor's home. Shit, it might be Betty. It sounded like glass breaking and doors being slammed shut. I was in full sprint now, racing right into the problem while looking left and right, scanning like a tank turret for threats. Several porch lights on my street illuminated in succession. Others heard it too. I thought, this is no damn nightmare. Instinctively, I reached for my patrol radio. Dammit, it's not here. My heart sank as I realized I didn't have a way to call for backup.

As I got closer to the home, I could see the screen door was ripped and a small window on the wooden door had been smashed. It appeared to be a home invasion. My heart jumped as I shook my head, angry because I was running out of time to save Betty. I stopped short of going into the house as I tried to catch my breath and listen for an indicator to pinpoint the location of the screaming. Then I heard voices arguing.

"You worthless woman! You thought you could take her away from me," a man yelled at someone, probably Betty. His voice cracked as he shouted. I'd heard people speak like that before. They've been enraged and homicidal. His screaming provided me cover as I scurried across the gravel walkway trying to see through the large bay window. Movement from the right caught my eye. I spun around and spotted a nosy neighbor shining a flashlight on me. I tried to wave her off. Wait, she could help. I mimicked using a telephone with my hand and fingers hoping she'd figure that I wanted her to call 911. She turned and scampered back toward her home, shaking her head at me as she entered the house. Doubtful she'll help.

Then I heard what sounded like a slap. "Leave me alone. This is your fault. She doesn't want to be with you, and I hate you!" Betty pleaded. I recognized her voice for sure that time. Something came over me and I feared she'd die if I didn't do something quick. Then I remembered her young daughter. The poor thing shouldn't have to go through this. My intuition and training said I should wait to see if someone called 911, but I carefully grabbed the door and tiptoed around broken glass and entered the house. It was humid inside, and the constant hum of an oscillating fan almost drowned out the radio playing in the background.

"You're never gonna get away with this. I'm leaving with her, and if you get in my way I'm gonna kill you," snarled the suspect. The anger in his voice stung and was convincing. I was positive he'd already decided what he wanted to do, and how he was going to accomplish it. The tiny hairs on the back of my neck stood straight up.

"That's not happening. You don't have the guts to shoot me," Betty screamed with conviction. Uh oh, she said "shoot" me. Son-of-a-bitch… he's got a gun. Things somehow just got worse, and I didn't think that was possible. Normal physical reactions to the stress resulted. Suddenly, my pulse quickened and sweat was beading on my forehead. My palms were becoming clammy and my gun began to feel heavier. Back and forth they argued. I knew he could kill her any second, but I wasn't sure what to do next. Move closer you coward, she needs you.

I poked my head around the corner and still couldn't see them. All the doors to the hallway on the right were shut, and I didn't see any light coming from the rooms. Since my eyes had adjusted to the low light, I could see two different ways into the kitchen. I wanted to surprise the suspect. If I could catch him off guard, I might be able to distract him long enough to rescue Betty. The hardwood floor creaked as I moved… and I froze. Uh oh. The arguing stopped and it sounded as though a single muffled voice was coming from the kitchen.

I burst around the corner and saw the suspect had his arm around Betty. He was covering her mouth with one hand. His other hand had a .357 magnum pressed up against her temple. The look in his eyes scared me because I could feel him looking right through me. Betty was shaking uncontrollably and my heart dropped.

"And who the hell are you? Her new boyfriend?" he said to me, then he looked at Betty. "You replaced me that fast, huh?"

"No, man. I'm her neighbor," I replied matter-of-factly. Since he was watching her, I saw a small opening and swung my gun up and aimed it right at his head.

"I'm a cop. Let her go. You don't need to do this, man. I know exactly how you feel," I blurted out.

He squeezed Betty even tighter and hit her head with his gun. "You picked the wrong day to be a hero, boy. Ain't anybody who knows how I feel." He looked around the kitchen, at me, at my gun pointed at him. He's searching for a way out.

"My wife just left me and took my kids. I sure the hell know what you're feeling, but this isn't the way to deal with it," I pleaded with him and shook my head. "Another neighbor called 911. This place is going to be crawling with cops any second." I lied while trying to confuse and stall him. My mind raced to figure out a way to save Betty, but in that moment, nothing seemed to be working.

The man snorted and shook his head. "I'm giving you five seconds to drop your gun." He pulled the hammer back on his revolver. "Or I shoot her." There was no doubt in my mind he would kill Betty. I had a split-second to consider my options, and I had none.

"One, two, three," he said and I couldn't stand the look in Betty's eyes. She had given up. But I hadn't. I lowered my gun. The suspect smiled wryly. He lowered his gun but didn't let Betty go. The suspect looked between

Betty and me several times. It seemed the wheels were turning in his sick head. Betty tried to shake free from his grasp. She looked to her left, and I couldn't be sure or not, but it appeared as if she just nodded. What the hell does that mean?

"Well, you ain't as dumb as you look. Problem is... I'm screwed either way." He snapped the gun back up, and I did the same. A bright flash was followed by a loud bang and ringing in my ears. I hadn't fired a round, neither had he. His skull fragments splintered to my left and Betty lunged forward. Man, what the hell just happened? I tried to assess the situation but was freaked out and running only on adrenaline.

Sirens graced my eardrums, and I rushed to comfort Betty. She was sobbing. "My baby, my baby," she said as she pointed toward the hallway but fell to the floor. No way, it couldn't be.

I carefully peeked around the corner. Betty's eleven-year-old daughter was standing there in her nightgown covered in her own father's blood. Her face was pale and she was trembling. She was holding a gun with two hands and crying. I looked back at Betty and saw she was trying to crawl towards us. Finally, I noticed blood on Betty's leg. She'd been shot. I lowered my gun, grabbed the phone from the wall and dialed 911. As I advised the call taker of the situation, I ran over to the little girl. I grabbed her and held her as if she were my own child. Then I carried her over to her mother.

Betty had been shot in the femoral artery. Her daughter continually whispered that she was sorry while holding her mom's hand. I searched Betty's leg wound for the damaged artery and squeezed it as hard as I could, hoping paramedics would get there soon. Sometime, I don't know when, a man reached over my shoulder, followed my fingers with his, and clamped the artery. He tapped me out and he and his partner began trying to save Betty. The sight of Betty's daughter covered in blood concerned them too. As she and her daughter were loaded into the ambulance, I watched and stared blankly at the back of it as it pulled away, thanking God I was still alive. I would have given anything to hold my own children at that moment, but I couldn't.

After giving a statement, I walked back to my home and took a cold shower. When I get out, I sat on my bed. The clock read 3:45 AM. I wasn't entirely sure why, but I cried myself to sleep. At some point, I woke up to the sound of someone knocking on my front door, and I labored to get out of bed. Who the hell's there? I glanced at the clock… 8:07 AM. I opened the door and saw my two children standing there, dressed, and ready for school. They also had large, stuffed duffle bags with them.

At the curb I saw my ex-wife approaching the front door. "We'll talk later. I hear you're off for a few weeks. The kids wanted to stay with you. You okay with that?" she asked. I could tell she was sincere and the offer was real. No more head games. I wanted to hug and kiss her, but instead I tried to play it cool.

"Sure thing. Thanks." I barely finished saying the words when my kids ran and jumped on me. They gave me hugs and kisses, and for a brief moment, I held the world in my arms. I cried again, but this time for the sheer joy.

Shooter

By Rick Smith

Complacency is, and will always be, one of the top reasons cops get killed. I tell this to my recruits every day while they attend the basic police academy. It's quite an anomaly being on the other side of the table with a bunch of fresh faced, doe-eyed, and still wet behind the ears rookies who haven't made it beyond the textbooks allegedly teaching them to be cops...but not how to survive. I once filled their shoes. I rose all the way to the rank of Detective before medically retiring. With every video I show them, there comes a loud 'gasp' in unison from these young adults- still eager to earn a badge, but far more cognizant of what they actually signed up for. These blue-bloods, who may one day pay the ultimate sacrifice for their career, remind me of how I almost lost my life while wearing a badge several years ago.

It was the summer of 2007, and everything about the day, especially the moment, seems like it happened last week. It was an unusually hot year, foreboding and full of tension in the air. It felt like someone had placed all of us in my small town of 30,000 into a deep pressure cooker, flipped the on switch, and waited for something, or someone, to inexplicably burst.

I began my career in my small town 2005, after several years working in corrections with the Inyo County Sheriff's Department, which began in 2002. By the time this event occurred in '07, I felt I was already a seasoned veteran of law enforcement. I felt, without a doubt, that I was "hot shit." But, I was about to be reminded of just how quickly life can turn upside down, everything can change in an instant, all in the blink of an eye. I recall the suspect's stare. He was hell bent on dying, and there wasn't any training, or video, or anything else we could do based on the situation.

After many years of internal playback surrounding the events of that day, I always go back to the smells. It's almost as if I was a rookie smelling a dead body for the first time. Once the confrontation happened, I never forgot the putrid stench that filled my nostrils and permeated every surface of my body with the emptiness and quiet of rotting human flesh. The smell after the shooting was of sulfur-a short lasting component of gunpowder. When released into the atmosphere from the barrel of a firearm, it adds a smoky smell in small enclosed spaces.

I remember even more vividly the moment because I had just returned from vacation. This was day one back at the detective bureau. I had enjoyed the last two weeks in my hometown of North Carolina, soaking up sun rays from the beach and feasting on local seafood and tangy Eastern N.C. barbeque. To say I was not prepared to return to the cop life was an understatement. So, the looming tragedy, just part of the job, was even more greatly magnified based on the fact I hadn't mentally prepared myself to be back to work.

The first call I received that morning was one from our service yard wanting my unmarked car in for service. Typically, when turning in a car for service, one emptied it out, removing all firearms and other personal items. However, on this particular day, *my* complacency got the better of me. I was about to make an egregious error that nearly made my wife a widow...and could have easily made many more wives widows.

I recall I had my typical Glock model 23 on my hip, but left my patrol rifle, an AR-15 in the trunk, with my 12-gauge police issue 12-gauge shotgun full of double-ot buckshot. The most important piece of equipment left in my unmarked was not a firearm that day, but my ballistic vest, which I typically didn't wear in the office being assigned to the detective bureau. I wasn't particularly worried about wearing it on this day because I had no plans to jump right back into the underbelly of the town I worked in. My original intent and plans for the day included combing case logs. Good detectives do that; they scrutinize casework from other cops in hopes of finding connections to other unsolved cases that they're working on. I consider myself a good cop. That was my plan, and that was what I was going to do until fate changed things.

If you've ever watched television, it isn't hard to imagine where I worked-a Midwest desert town named, Ridgecrest. There's nothing for kids to do to keep themselves entertained. Couple that with a growing methamphetamine problem and you have a place that can make a person crack if you don't have a clear sense of purpose. Get stuck out in the streets without any education or background and the easiest cheapest way to get money is to sell dope. I've never quite understood the psychology behind methamphetamine as it turns ordinary everyday people into jabbering dirty shells of their former selves.

I was in the office maybe a few hours reviewing reports when I heard the dispatcher come over the radio. When you're familiar with your dispatchers as we are in smaller agencies, you can interpret a sense of urgency from the tone of voice the dispatcher uses. It can be one that carries a sense of urgency or one that means 'take your time.' This particular call immediately raised my pulse and adrenaline as I detected fear and angst, two qualities that are rarely ever heard in a dispatcher's voice.

The call: "All units, active shooter in progress, Southern Sierra Medical Plaza."

I was the first to respond via radio and ran to my unmarked police car to begin the mile drive north to the hospital. I exceeded 110 mph, because upon arrival my car nearly blew the engine from overheating. I was happy to have made it alive considering I knew I drove as fast as possible through lunchtime traffic to arrive on scene first. I popped my trunk to grab some gear and then cursed.

"Forgot my shit, I muttered."

I had my Glock 23 on my hip with one magazine in it, no vest, and a can of pepper spray in my pocket. The only other thing I was carrying was my handcuffs. I stood by waiting for cover units and heard a loud boom come from inside the clinic. I proceeded to make my way to the side of the building as I surveyed the scene on arrival and noticed mirrored glass on the front entrance door. As I made my way to the side of the clinic, I heard another loud boom. This time screaming followed. Several other patrol units pulled in and we gathered at my location. There were six of us...a perfect size for an entry team. It never crossed out minds that running into an active shooter situation would change some of us forever.

We approached the side door, it burst open and nurses poured out like ants from an anthill. I'll never forget their faces or the screaming. It was utter chaos, and had it not been for excellent training and professional lawmen with excellent trigger control, one of us cops could have easily shot one of those frightened nurses while panicking or assuming they were a suspect.

As we entered the building being assaulted, the smell of sulfur and the eerie view of smoke in the air from the shooter met our eyes and noses. We all noticed the hallways were extremely narrow. Had the shooter popped around any one of the corners, he could have easily taken out two or three of us with a single blast. I felt numb at this point, and I was terrified thinking this was going to be my last day on this planet. I hadn't said goodbye to my wife and kids when I left for work this morning, and the thought irritated me immensely.

The hallway in front of us was next to deal with. Suddenly, another deafening blast shook the building. It was definitely a shotgun blast. Screams covered the echoes from the round going off. We entered an office from the rear, and saw a glass door directly in front of us. It led to a waiting room. The glass door had a broken 'spider web' pattern from being shot through at close range.

Unbeknownst to us at the time, was the fact that an idiot Sergeant had entered through the front door, which I determined was not a viable entry point because the lead man would have no view of what threat he was walking into. Once we neared the glass door, we saw a dark figure carrying a shotgun on the other side. We could not tell what the shooter was doing, however. I raised my gun and prepared to shoot the suspect dead.

Prior to shooting the shadowy subject, I heard the person yell, "Drop the gun!" I knew instantly it was not a suspect, but rather the Sergeant who'd decided to take over the call without letting anyone know.

All I could think to myself was, "Dipshit's gonna get killed." Then again, I was no better. I was the idiot without a ballistic vest...during an active shooter!

We figured out quickly that the Sergeant had the shooter at gunpoint on the other side of the wall. The stack of guys in order consisted of my CHP counterpart, me, and several others. Among the group was also my best friend, a man I went to the police academy with.

We opened the door and swung around the corner. I remember hearing my CHP partner order the guy to drop the gun as well. I looked and saw the shooter, an old man, probably in his seventies. He had the shotgun pointed down and was looking directly into our eyes. My partner again ordered him to drop the gun. I have never considered myself clairvoyant by any stretch of the imagination. This day though, I saw the acceptance of death on his face and in his eyes, and I knew what was about to happen. The empty coldness of his deep blue eyes haunted me then and continues to stay with me.

The suspect slowly raised the gun and my friend fired once into the suspect's lower abdomen. I didn't know this until I attended the shooters autopsy the next day, but two of the pellets from my partner's shotgun struck the subject directly in his spine causing him to fall to the floor face first and killing him.

I fell down, drawing out my handcuffs, and secured the subject's hands behind his back. I didn't even feel his blood on my hands until someone pointed it out a few minutes later. Oddly enough, I noticed my ears weren't ringing as they normally did on the range when I forgot to put on hearing protection prior to firing my weapon. I had been less than two feet from where my partner's gun went off and my hearing was normal. I later learned that the body compensates for hearing when involved in a shooting as a form of protection.

I learned many things that day. I learned how quickly we can become involved in life and death scenarios, even in small towns. I learned that people, no matter what age, are capable of horrifying behavior. But, more tragically, I came to understand that wearing the badge and handling calls leads to years of restless nights full of nightmares. I'm left wondering when, or if, the nightmares ever end.

Forgotten Warriors

By Sherrill L. Swinney

As dawn broke on a warm humid day off the coast of North Vietnam, I sat at my General Quarters position. We were about to attack the Haiphong Harbor area of the Do Son Peninsula. In an effort to stop the supply chain from the sea to the port, and from the port to the troops in the north, the job of the Naval destroyers was to use their five-inch 54 Guns to destroy bridges, roads, gun batteries, and other designated targets, as well as to fire harassing and interdicting missions. There were several destroyers, including a couple of guided missile capable destroyers, on this mission. We were there to take out the shore batteries, any small boat attacks, and the nearby bridges and ammunition dumps.

Since the mission was being conducted in daylight, it was more dangerous for obvious reasons. The enemy's use of surface-to-air missiles had improved limiting our air support capabilities.

Nevertheless, our job was to be a diversion so that the planes could mine the harbor to cut off the supplies to the north. My duty station for General Quarters was in the Combat Information Center (CIC) watching a radar scope and listening to radio communications.

The silence was broken by a Flash message over the secure radio circuit.

"Parkland, this is War eagle. Proceed to point X-ray. Turn to course 045 degrees and commence firing."

"This is Parkland. Roger. Out!" was the reply.

The war, for the day, was on. We maintained this firing course for thirty minutes. We then made a turn to 180 degrees to return while the North Vietnamese were raining down a barrage of 152 millimeter shells where we'd just been.

With expert maneuvering by the skipper and crew on the bridge, we were able to steer into the most recent splash points of enemy shells and avoid being hit. We escaped with no major damage or loss of life. We'd live to fight another day, but couldn't shake how we were unappreciated fighters in an unpopular war. Still, this is the life of a forgotten warrior.

Then next day we had Notification Line duties, where we warned merchant vessels that Haiphong Harbor had been mined. The following day, we were back to the gun line to start a four day run. During this time, we participated in sixty seven naval gunfire strike missions, twenty of which were opposed by hostile fire from the North Vietnamese. We worked twenty hour days during this time, firing our guns from 4000 yards offshore to 1000 yards from the beach. We then steamed out to sea to find refueling and rearming ships to get ready for the next mission.

Our skipper, Captain Deal, required the ship's cooks to prepare and serve four meals a day to keep us fed and awake and ready to fight.

We were a group of men from all parts of the United States who had one common goal. We'd raised our hands in honor and we'd sworn to love and defend our country...even in the midst of an unpopular war. Some had joined voluntarily while many were drafted, but we all served with honor.

What we came home to was another terrible story of mistreatment and misunderstanding. This is a quote from the Commander, Destroyer Squadron Nine, in May, 1972.

"A proud, confident, well trained, informed and high spirited crew...fired 3,417 rounds in 19 days... averaged one gun up 100% of the time...02 guns up 95% never failing to deliver required rounds in target area...engaged three firing CD sites in a single mission, firing 484 rounds counter-battery fire during retirement...never on water hours...R.S. Edwards is among the very few...."

This was all the "Kudos" we'd get after we served as his flag ship for three weeks in May 2, 1972.

One Hundred Eighteen

By Ian Snyder

One hundred and eighteen men and women in law enforcement woke up on January 1, 2014, looking forward to another year of selflessly serving their communities. What these brave souls did not know, was that this year would be their last. Some would lose their lives to car accidents, some to health issues while on duty, but many fell from a much worse fate...that of being murdered by evil monsters. Ironically killed by the same monsters they swore to defend others from...villains who'd even killed innocent community members.

This evil is something most people choose to dismiss since they don't see it on a regular basis, and they'll likely never experience it. However, it's what we in law enforcement see every day. Most of you would get sick to your stomach if you saw what we saw, lived what we lived through...many of you would turn your heads in disgust or dismay. But not the brave souls who lost their lives in the line of duty; or the men and women who put on their uniforms every day, kiss their loved ones, and report to duty knowing the cards are stacked against them. We do it because it's a calling. It's in our blood, and truth be told, there's not much more in the way of a profession that we should be doing.

The one hundred and eighteen brothers and sisters who lost their lives in 2014 did so with honor and dignity. They gave the ultimate sacrifice to keep the rest of the country safe. These brave souls, as well as all law enforcement officers, ask very little from the communities they serve. We ask that people obey the laws, return respect once given, and above all, let us do our job without interference and ridicule for doing so. We want to make it home safely to our families at the end of our shift just like everyone else does.

When you see a police officer driving in their patrol car, on the side of the road assisting a stranded motorist or stopping someone, or at a call, remember the officer's that have lost their lives doing the same thing, and remember that they are human. We cry, bleed, sweat, and live like everyone else. Remember that, it's important.

As the times change, laws change, and the President Of The United States forms committees to suggest how police should do their jobs, we will work hard to adapt and provide the very highest level of service we can to the community. We make mistakes, but we learn from them. We want to succeed and be an intricate part of the community.

I end with a quote, one to honor the men and women who lost their lives, and all the blue blooded brothers and sisters pushing a patrol car, taking reports, rescuing people, and manning the front lines of peace:

Matthew 5:9 *"Blessed are the peacemakers, for they shall be called the children of God."*

Never Forget Our Fallen

By Harriet Fox

I remember the first time I stood at a policeman's funeral. It was his end of watch moment. The year was 1998, and I vowed I would never forget that man.

I remember amongst thousands of officers on a gloomy, almost drizzly City of Angels day, standing at attention on the cemetery lawn. I was struggling to comprehend how this could happen. His wife and two children had lost their father and husband. A police department had lost their partner and friend.

It was in this moment I realized, police officers die for the uniform they wear. Realizing this, without thought, I vowed I would always wear a uniform. While I am not a police officer working the streets today, I do wear a uniform and do risk my life every time I put my uniform on.

We had just come from a massive church where I watched the funeral service via monitors in the overflow standing room only area outside of the church's place of worship. I stood there young and in the beginning years of my law enforcement career.

I thought about this police officer in the locker room getting ready at the beginning of his shift on that final day. I thought about him, foot perched on the locker room bench, as he laced up his black polished boots, staring down at my own.

Did he ever think about the possibly this could be his last time he may be lacing up those boots or putting his Sam Brown at his hips? *I doubt it.* He was planning his wife's surprise birthday party for the next day. I am sure his mind was excited about that upcoming day. But instead of having her party that Friday, his wife grieved the loss of her husband and father of her children.

Sadly since that 1998 day, I have been to many cops' funerals. Too many that is. Not one funeral had less than thousands of officers. The camaraderie, support, and brotherhood always showed prevalent. The founder of the *Officer Down Memorial Page* has a quote that sums it up: *"When a police officer is killed, it's not an agency that loses an officer, it's an entire nation."* Officers come from around the nation and from other countries to pay their respects. That's a big deal.

And through the almost twenty years on the job, attending the memorial services of these men, I never forgot any of them. I vowed I would help keep their memory alive by doing just that: remembering them.

I have and always will.

Statistics show an officer dies in the line of duty every 58 hours in the United States. It seems the fallen are falling faster than I experienced before. At least it feels this way.

Violence is rampant every day, everywhere. Ambushes and suicide-by-cop assaults are on the rise. Police officers risk their lives every single day to protect their cities, towns, and communities.

We know the risk of the job. It's what we signed up for. We all sign up for this job knowing we deal with evil and that at any time we could be harmed. We choose the risk. But we do not expect it. Our plan is always to go home at the end of the day. And every law enforcement officer deserves to go home. Unfortunately, this plan sometimes does not play out.

When a police officer is killed, the anger, we as a law enforcement family feel, is raw and real. Sadness, fear, and shock are just a few emotions thrown into the equation. But through all this, there's always a huge sense of pride.

Someone gave their life supporting what they believed in while trying to help others for a greater cause. They helped and kept people safe every day while serving.

Our fallen comrades committed the most selfless act every time they were on the job, not just that final day. They are heroes.

Qualities of a hero include: sacrifice, determination, loyalty, courage, dedication, and conviction. Officers are saving lives, helping the needy, and responding to emergencies daily. They are putting their health and safety on the line for the welfare of people they do not even know. They spend their working hours dealing with everyone else's problems. They spend more time at work than home with their loved ones.

Time is never enough in life. Time with our fallen was definitely not enough. They were taken away too soon. They were heroes to those who knew them before they were taken away and they became heroes to those of us who attended their funerals. Each service has their audience walking away feeling like they knew them. Almost feeling as if they were friends.

I have come to realize the only thing that allows it all to make sense to me. The thing that helps us accept this tragic misfortune is that our fallen comrades are truly the ultimate warriors who made the ultimate sacrifice.

It can feel like their deaths are senseless, but they are not. They died for what they loved doing and for protecting and serving. Their deaths are not in vain. These officers died defending the people of their community. These officers put their lives on the line so that others do not have to. The righteousness and standing up to evil is in their core. These officers will have not died in vain, but instead in death before dishonor.

When duty calls, we find ourselves standing at another funeral, paying our last respects. We owe it to these heroes to never forget them.

The funeral programs ride shotgun in my glove box stacked one on top of the other from all the funerals I have attended. As I lace my boots up at the beginning of shift and place my badge on my heart, I pretend to wear these for all the men and women who died doing what they loved. I live my life in their honor.

And I do know, I will never forget.

Barometer

By Denise Spiller

It was 1992, and I was assigned to the Women's Correctional center as a correctional officer. By this time, having been a C/O since 1989, I had just enough experience to feel comfortable. Comfortable enough to feel like I had a handle on the emotional side of the job. Comfortable enough to slip up and let my guard down just enough to be a disappointment to myself. After all, I had a standard.

Most of us know that annoying little thing. It is the moral barometer we carry with us that sets the tone for our lives and daily journey. Sometimes it gets a little heavy. Sometimes it gets damaged. And if we are being completely honest here, sometimes that damn thing just gets in the way.

This would be one of those times.

An old timer deputy set the tone that shift. He had at least 15 years under his belt and was a little more than pissed off. Pissed off that a girl, over 300 pounds, had made him run. She was a thief. And she was not in the mood to come back to jail on this particular night, so she ran.

She only made it half a block, but as he told the story to me and my partner while booking her into custody, he was pissed. His forehead still had tiny beads of sweat and he was still slightly winded. His collar was folded up and it was apparent she took him for a run that night.

As the deputy was sharing his ordeal he exclaimed, "Fat bitch made me fucking chase her!" We looked at him and then each other. "Does my fat ass look like it wants to be running?!"

Rhetorical question, of course.

"Did she honestly think she was not getting arrested tonight? Fucking fat ass!" He shook his head and sighed deeply. My partner and I looked at each other again. It was one of those moments when you do not know if it is okay to laugh. There was a moment of silence and then we both burst out with laughter that we had been trying to hold in. We knew this deputy. And that was damn funny!

The humor on this job is quite different from other fields. Things seen, stories told, surprising moments, there is always something. Not a week of work could go by without some humorous or surprising story. And this night was one for the memory books.

The deputy continued to ramble on, "Fuck you guys, shit ain't funny! See how much you're laughing when you gotta search her! She's hiding something, a few somethings maybe! I think she has at least a wallet, maybe a credit card, so the jokes on you!" I stopped laughing and glanced over at the arrestee through the glass of the cell door window.

I could see through the small window that she too was sweaty and still panting a bit. She really was a large woman. Tall, wide, and quite obese. This was not going to be fun. She looked mad. I decided in that moment, this search would be a two-person search for safety precautions and good measure.

What happened next made an impression on me that I would not soon forget! Here I am talking about it years later, so therefore the impression was everlasting. I believed this was the first search where I experienced conflicting emotions. In fact, this may have been feelings I had felt for the first time in my adult life. Something started to gnaw at me.

I felt many things ... but mostly, what remained was shame and disappointment because as we laughed about her fat and stink, I knew better. I had a feeling she could hear us and I felt like we should have had more compassion, have been more professional, and just been more humane.

But I said nothing. I stood by and played along. I kept

giggling, too. In my mind, I did not stand up for what was right. It was then I entered the holding cell to begin the search.

First step in and the odor still remains and is quite unforgettable. There was a combination of sweat, funk, old socks, and melted fat. She had at least 3-4 rolls and we had to instruct her to lift each roll up so we could see. She defended her right to not help us, but of course we insisted. She just stood there. She didn't resist, but she also didn't follow our instructions. She stood in silent resistance and forced us to do what we dreaded yet knew we must do.

We separated, raised, lifted, and pulled apart every roll. By the time the search was over, we had recovered a brown wallet and two credit cards that she had purposely hid by lodging them between her rolls. They were sweaty and sticky, they smelled awful, and she was horribly ashamed. This was a first for me; inmates do hide things in their fat rolls! Throughout my career I would come to find that a desperate person will hide just about anything anywhere on or in their body.

This was only night one for her. She spent months in jail and with every single opportunity, she fought and fought and fought. Any chance she had, it seems that she was fighting over any and every small thing. I separated many fights that included her. She was moved to different rooms, then different housing units, and eventually made her way to the one-woman cell where she would be alone.

I knew that she was fighting over more than the petty issues inmates fight about in jail. And I remember feeling a bit of shame myself, because I realized from the moment she likely heard us laughing, that she was fighting for her right to be fat and not made fun of. She was fighting for the biggest thing in her life, her dignity.

Even years later, in a wheelchair, one or two of her kids putting money on her books -she was still running her scam, still being a thief, still cheating life and I, her polar opposite, took that encounter and chose to grow, to change, to mature. I think it is ironic an inmate taught me something of great value about life when she herself chose not to learn or grow or change. She continued, for nearly the decade that I worked the women's jail, to play the victim. She chose to stay that particular course, one that would lead her to a life of endless health problems and nights in jail.

This situation, one that taught me a valuable life lesson, made me turn to my moral barometer more often and actually listen to it. This was one of those lessons about being true to myself. To get my attitude and own behavior in check, and define my course rather than let others define it for me. What I did not do then, I do now. I stay true to my own nature, true to my own intent, and I hold a standard of behavior I can be proud of.

This is law enforcement. Sometimes we unknowingly give up a piece of ourselves when we choose this industry.

Control what you can and hold on to your truest self.   In the
end, this is all you have.

How Did I Get Here?

By David Kettering

So how, at the dawn of ones 5th decade on this orb, after attaining a degree in Meteorology and then working in the electronics business for 23-plus years, does one end up working in a correctional facility, meeting and dealing with all kinds of people who are not at their best? The short answer is that I needed to find employment after being laid off during an economic downturn in the semiconductor industry...by a company where I'd worked for 20 years. I definitely needed employment, but in a correctional facility? Obviously, either some severe mental illness forced ill-advised decisions or the universe was playing some cruel joke on me. And perhaps, just perhaps, life experiences over the past four decades were intended to steer me towards working night shift in a dark correctional facility filled with people I never thought I would encounter. Ever.

Nevertheless, here I am. It's strange and, at times, frightening. It's sometimes disconcerting and sometimes it's disgusting. But it's always interesting. Unlike my previous careers, where I constantly dealt with the same people and the activity from day to day did not vary greatly, each day in the jail is unique. I never know who's coming through the intake door or how people, inmates and co-workers, are going to behave from day to day. Yeah, some of the inmates became pretty predictable, but each day offered new, or at least ever-changing, experiences.

By the time you're 50-plus, you kind of figure that you have seen it all and that you can handle whatever comes your way. After all, you've made it this far. However, there is nothing that prepares you for people strung out on drugs, detoxing from alcohol, "tweaking" after being on meth for a few days, playing with their own excrement, or hiding things in various body orifices. Exactly how does a guy decide that filling a piece of bicycle inner tube with tobacco, rolling papers, and a lighter before sticking it up his rear end is a good idea? Why does a certain female inmate like to write on the wall with her own feces? A pencil would have been easier to read, easier to clean off, and a lot less stinky.

What the heck am I doing here? I don't want to see these things. But these people are real. The things they do are real. Their problems are real. How can there be so many people like this? Then I noticed these people like to talk. They want to tell you about their pain, their problems, their families, their friends, their children, their cars, their girlfriends, and their wives. They don't expect you to solve their problems. They just want to talk. Should I listen?

That question initially caused some internal conflict. I'm tasked with ensuring the safety and security of the facility, my co-workers, and the inmates. I'm not here to be a friend to the inmates or to show favoritism to anyone. However, in order to ensure the safety and security of the facility, my co-workers, and the inmates, I need to know what's going on with them. What better way to know what's going on than to listen? So I started listening. A lot. The more I listened, the easier it was to interact with and manage the inmates. The more I listened, the more they listened when I told them to do something. The internal conflict and distress, that I had initially felt, disappeared like an extra tray at chow time.

It seems that, in fact, previous life experiences dealing with people had prepared me for precisely this profession. I work in a facility filled with people who are troubled, sometimes violent, sometimes bizarre, and they're lawbreakers. But, they are also people. As each of us travels the pathways of our lives, we come in contact with thousands of other people. Some we meet many times, some we meet a few times, and many we meet only once. Regardless of who we meet, how many times we meet, and the circumstances under which we meet, each interaction we have with another person has an effect. It has an effect on the other person and it has an effect on us. Whether that effect boosts upward in a positive direction or drags down towards despair can be a conscious decision. Do we decide to view these interactions as a necessary evil and part of the job, or do we decide to view them as an opportunity to have a positive influence on another human being?

I choose the latter. And it turned out to be one of the best decisions I've ever made. A situation that I never imagined being in, has turned into one that has been unbelievably rewarding. I relish the prospect of new challenges and new interactions every day. The inmates that I judged so harshly in the beginning have turned out to be other human beings with human problems like everyone else. Demonstrating a small amount of human compassion by listening to an inmate results in tremendous return for me on an emotional and job satisfaction standpoint. And that feels great. If an inmate benefits from talking with me or even watching the way that I do my job, then that is an added benefit. A job that I initially wondered was right for me has turned into a career that I know I'm right for. And that's a win in anyone's book.

Many people hear the word "corrections" and immediately think of either the many reality shows dealing with jails and prisons or of the several movies featuring "lock-up" scenes. They tend to think of brutish "guards" manhandling inmates. They think of inmates peering out like so many caged animals in a zoo from rows of cells with metal bars. They think of hellish living conditions in rooms overcrowded with bunk beds. And they think of poorly prepared food slopped onto metal trays and eaten in a large, dangerous dining hall. Before I walked into the jail where I began my corrections career, I entertained similar misconceptions. Reality, I found, can be much different than the stereotypical version portrayed by the media for mass consumption.

While some older prison facilities may still have rows of cells with metal bars, any facility constructed in the past thirty years has cells with doors made of metal or wood. The vast majority of correctional staff members are decent people doing a difficult job with the intent of going home safely at the end of their shift. There are building standards in place in California that dictate what features a correctional facility must have. The rights of inmates are also codified from how many calories per day of food they receive to how much time they must have outside of their cell. The living conditions in my place of employment, while not luxurious, are certainly tolerable. Inmates are provided three square meals a day, all prescribed medications, clean clothing, a bed, and free television. Just like a resort! Except, you can't leave when you want, and breakfast is at 4:00 A.M. And your toilet is located in your bedroom. And you can't select your roommate. OK, it's not quite like a resort.

What makes corrections so interesting to me is the variety of people and events I encounter each day. The co-workers on my team are from many backgrounds, educational levels, and age groups, but as different as we all are, we're like a family. We have each other's back and we work hard to make sure we all go home. Like any family there may be disagreements and some petty jealousies, but when you need them, they're there. Did a fight just kick-off on your housing pod? The cavalry comes pouring onto the housing pod, ready for anything. It's a comforting feeling to know that you have the full support of your teammates when you're working in a dangerous environment. It's also rewarding to have so many people interested in you doing your best work because they are depending on you. This dynamic encourages teaching your fellow workers and having an open mind to learn from them. This can be quite different from the highly competitive and, at times, cutthroat private sector where "whatever makes me look good" is the perceived way to the top.

Dealing with inmates on a daily basis is always challenging and entertaining. The inmates constantly try to manipulate you while, at the same time, you're trying to manipulate them. They want more time out of their cell, additional food, extra clothing, more time on the phone, access to contraband, their friend as a cell mate, and the ability to participate in gang activity. They play "games" to distract you while another does something behind your back. Meanwhile, you try to prevent all of these things. While constantly on full-alert, you must monitor gang participation, fights, bullying, "cheeking" medication, stealing, and escape attempts. Plus ensure "normal" housing pod activities such as court appointments, medical appointments, inmate visits, mail, inmate requests, changes in inmate housing location, programs like AA and NA, church services, laundry exchange, razor distribution and collection, and meals. Busy, challenging, mentally engaging, and constantly changing are a few words that come to mind. Whether you go home frustrated or feeling fulfilled and like you accomplished something depends upon who wins the "manipulation game."

Corrections isn't just "guarding" the bad guys. The jail is a process that begins when an officer brings the lawbreaker in the door. The offender must be searched, photographed, and fingerprinted. He must be medically cleared, his property inventoried, and his booking information entered into the jail database. He must be interviewed by the Intake Classification Officer, dressed into jail clothing, have his own clothing boxed, labeled, and placed into storage, and be given bedding and a hygiene kit. Once being escorted to his housing pod and listening to an orientation talk, the inmate is assigned a bunk. All of these activities are handled by correctional staff assigned to each area. It usually goes smoothly but, every now and then, you get a person who just really doesn't want to participate in the process in a cooperative manner. By every now and then I mean pretty much every day. It's not pretty, it gets people hurt, and this is where the reality shows most closely represent reality. It's also where teamwork and professionalism come into play. We know how to anticipate aberrant behavior and how to circumvent it or effectively and safely handle it. Everyone eventually gets through the intake process.

At the other end of the jail process comes the release process. Inmates can be released from custody outright, released to prison, a drug treatment program, or sent to another agency. Paperwork is crucial here. The person must be sent to the right place or released correctly. We have many homeless or destitute inmates who have little to no belongings once released. The genuine look of thanks you receive by handing them a bus pass or article of clothing donated by the community is immensely rewarding. Being able to participate in these moving moments is one of the things that get me through some of the rough shifts we have.

Corrections is a mentally and physically challenging career, one filled with constant opportunities working with real people. Making a difference positively in these people's lives keeps me coming back each day.

Ambush (Fiction)

By C. L. Swinney

The bullet grazed my temple leaving a thin blood trail trickling down my cheek. Instinctively I dove for cover behind a vehicle and reached for my handgun. Damn that was close! I scanned the alley for the shooter while checking my wound with my free hand. Ambient light from the street pole revealed fresh blood, my blood, and I decided I was not going to die. There was no image of my wife or kids flashing in my mind. I didn't say a prayer. The only thing I saw was a poorly lit alley, and all I wanted to do was kill the son-of-a-bitch who'd just shot me. My heart pounded in my chest. I finally exhaled after realizing I'd been holding my breath far too long.

"Come on out piggy!" yelled the suspect. He fired off more rounds wildly in my direction. It was a catastrophic mistake for him. Now, based on his voice and the muzzle flash, I had a much better idea where he was hiding. I reached for my radio microphone to request cover units; however, my dive for cover had crushed it. The emergency button was lit indicating it still had power. I pressed it with my non-gun hand. My exact location was now displayed to dispatch. Gotta love GPS, I thought.

"Listen buddy, the troops are coming. Give up, and save yourself," I answered back. I didn't think he'd follow my lawful order, but it was the only words that came out of my mouth. I felt secure in my hiding spot since I wasn't getting hit by his sporadic gunfire, so for the moment, I was hunkered down.

"Fuck em' all! I'll get as many of you pricks as I can before I let you end it all for me!" Again he fired off more rounds at me. I cringed and fired back when my brain registered his statement. It's a damn suicide by cop, and I have no way to warn my backup. I was instantly deflated. If this went bad, a lost soul was going to die.

"You don't need to do this, put down the gun and we'll work this out." I felt a strong sense of trying to help him even though he was trying to kill me. Sounds weird, but it's what we do. Plus, he had me pinned down, and desperation forced me to try to negotiate. I was also trying to buy more time. Why I chose to try to rationalize with a man I knew clearly was not thinking straight was beyond me. He responded with a flurry of bullets. Dammit, he wants to die.

I peered under the vehicle I was hiding behind and could see he was basically trapped at the end of the alley. Solid structures surrounded him, accept he could get free if he came right by me, and that wasn't happening. This was going down in the industrial area of town, which meant my cover cars, even with full lights and sirens would be a bit longer before they made it. Bullets flew as I calculated my next move. Suddenly, I felt a sharp burning pain in my shoulder as one of his careless rounds hit me. I yelled out in pain and rolled over on my back. Are you kidding me, a damn ricochet! The pain was unbearable, like a thousand needles gouging at an open wound, but I had to continue. I inched closer behind a wheel and squeezed my trigger slowly and methodically while aiming at the area his muzzle flashes were coming from. The sound was deafening as dust and debris flew into my eyes. *Where the hell is my backup?*

I reloaded my firearm with my last magazine and tried to listen. My ears rang, making it difficult to hear. The wound in my shoulder throbbed and I could see it was bleeding badly. I strained to hear something as I considered, only briefly, that I might not survive. I counted rounds that I'd shot in my head and realized I was almost out. I glanced at my patrol vehicle. It was out in the open. If I made a move for it, the suspect would have a clear shot at me.

In a sadistic voice the suspect said, "Is that all you got? Boy, I served in the Marines!" He fired a couple rounds, "you ain't shit!" I rolled my eyes and was pissed. Obviously I hadn't hit him with my bullets, and it seemed like all I was doing was making him more mad. Compounding the issue was he'd just said he was a marine. I'd read how these guys suffer from PTSD and no one in the government wants to acknowledge or talk about it. They feel helpless, many times they are, and now one of them wants me, and all my friends, dead. A sick mind is caustic.

"Of all the luck," I huffed under my breath. I gotta do something, I thought.

I pleaded, "Man, you don't need to do this. We'll get you help, just throw down the gun and come out with your hands up." I felt awkward trying to reason with him, but I didn't see another option. My training, and overwhelming need to help, kicked in. I struggled with what I should do next. Then I wondered how I was going to pull it off. And then I heard it. Police sirens. *About damn time*, I thought as my eyes lit up and flickered.

"You don't know shit! Sounds like my welcoming party is almost here! I'll see you assholes in hell!" He fired a whole magazine toward me. Bullets slammed into the car that I was using as cover, and the bricks just to my right exploded. I tried to return fire, but felt helpless. Don't give up. Then the shooting stopped. I assumed he was reloading. In the eerie silence, two police cruisers skidded to a halt behind me, and positioned their cars to block the alley.

"Suicide by cop! I need medics!" I yelled at the two guys jumping out from their patrol cars. It's a situation in which shooting and killing someone is justified, but I thought if it were me, I'd want to know the situation I was responding to. "One shooter, far end on the left, heavily armed," I wanted to say more, but the suspect began shooting at the two officers, pelting their cars with rounds. They had to return fire in an effort to stop the threat while looking for better cover. I looked at my arm and could see the bleeding had clotted. It felt numb and I was getting scared now.

With the shooter concentrated on them, I finally had an opening. I tried to push myself up to get to my patrol car, but my wounded arm buckled. With my gun still aimed down the alley, I managed to sort of roll over and get up. I wrangled my keys from my duty belt and was able to get the car trunk open. I could see my less than lethal shotgun, but bypassed it for an assault rifle. We were taking rounds, and I was injured. I grabbed and loaded the rifle. It was time to end this.

More police cars flooded the area. The suspect continued firing from behind a dumpster. He was shooting at me and the other two officers in what seemed like a never ending supply of bullets. The SWAT team was summoned, but the fact the guy was shooting randomly, at cops, I figured he wouldn't last another minute or so. We stopped to reload our guns and I froze because I could see the man walking out from behind the dumpster. He'd stopped shooting, and I noticed he was wearing a ballistic vest. Then I saw the handgun in his right hand. He ripped off the ballistic vest revealing military fatigues. We made eye contact. I thought I'd see fear and sadness, or maybe confusion in his eyes. I was wrong. All I saw was utter rage. He winked at me, and raised his gun. I could see an officer to my left who was having trouble with his gun and the suspect had him lined up in his sights. Without thought, just a reaction, I shot. It was over in an instant. I shook my head. I collapsed and lay on the street looking straight up at the stars. Then the sirens, barking dogs, and spinning helicopter blades faded into silence.

Far From Routine (Fiction)

By C. L. Swinney

Deputy Sheriff Smith arrived to work carrying his work boots and weathered ballistic vest. His damn locker combination didn't work, and the bastard he couldn't fathom working with again was standing naked a few lockers down flaunting his steroid-laden physique. Smith slammed his boots and vest on the floor, "Big deal, I'd still scrape the floor with you," he muttered a little too loud under his breath.

"What was that?" asked "Beefcake" while he strolled over to Smith pounding his chest like a low-land silverback gorilla. He stood mere inches from Smith, invading his personal space cushion, and clenched his fists as if he was trying to squish oranges into juice. Bustling and murmurs in the locker room slipped away, scurried to the shadows, clinging to the walls anxious for drama.

"I said big deal, I'd still scrape the floor with you," Smith answered defiantly. He'd had it with Beefcake, his job, he'd just received a text from his wife talking about divorce, and he hadn't even had his Peet's coffee yet. *To hell with them all.* He bladed himself to Beefcake preparing for a physical altercation.

Beefcake kicked Smith's gear out of the way and stepped even closer. His pride and integrity had been challenged by Smith's comment, and he couldn't let it go. The other gorillas would call him out and his place at the top of "Idiot Mountain" would be threatened if he let this comment slide. He telegraphed his next move while winking at Smith just before trying to punch him in the jaw. Smith ducked as Beefcake's fist rammed into Smith's locker. The others noticed a sergeant walk into the locker room and grabbed Beefcake and Smith while trying to break up the pissing contest. Some of the remaining men snickered hoping Smith would pummel Beefcake because no one liked a hot-shot.

As the sergeant walked into the gladiator arena between two rows of ancient lockers, he raised an eyebrow after noticing Beefcake was naked. He looked him up and down, pointed at his groin, and chuckled. Beefcake turned red in the face while the others realized they were still hugging a naked man. Just before they let him go, Smith's locker magically popped open.

Smith grinned and looked at Beefcake. "Thanks 'Fonzy.'" The room erupted in laughter and the tension exited as quickly as a parolee would after hearing, "Police search warrant!" Smith and Beefcake exchanged glances.

"You good?" Smith asked Beefcake.

He nodded. "Yup, see you out there." Two grown men, one still naked, shook hands and the force was back to normal.

Now they suited up for the real battle. The one where a punch to the jaw would be much better than what potentially waits for them. A treacherous environment full of guns, dope, gang members, robbers, killers, villains...not to mention the crazies plotting and training every single day to kill a cop or deputy. *If only I could get the opportunity*, Smith considered as he laced his boots tight and donned his mangy ballistic vest.

After briefing, Smith, Beefcake, and the rest of the team went their separate ways. Some have traffic details, others have meetings, Beefcake's headed to see one of his lady friends, and Smith rolls to Peet's coffee. They had twelve more hours to go. If they survived, they'd get to go home...some to happy homes, some to not-so-happy homes. For most of them, work is an escape. It's an extremely difficult job, but the stress at home, with family, mortgages, kids, bills, and the rest of it was like a pressure cooker for them. Sometimes these guys became ticking-time bombs.

Routine, if there's such a thing, patrol continued without too much excitement. There was a parking complaint on Middlefield, and a fifteen year old girl was reported missing. The dispatcher sent Smith to the missing child call and he rolled his eyes. He assumed she would be off with her boyfriend *and let me guess, her parents don't like her boyfriend.* He chuckled as it seems he's going to be in the middle of yet another pissing contest. Beefcake was sent to the parking complaint. He didn't respond. "Imagine that," Smith said out loud. *Hopefully the sergeant tracks him down.*

Smith drove to the location of the missing child report. On the way, he stopped at a red light. For some reason he noticed a lowered Cadillac in his side and rear view mirrors. It was occupied by four people, and it was slowly pulling up next to him. A red flag in his head was hoisted, and he went from condition orange to condition red. He heard and felt hip-hop music and saw the juveniles and young adults in the car were dressed in red. Instantly he classified them as gang members, and wondered why the younger ones weren't in school.

They inched closer to Smith. There was a lot of discussion and pointing coming from the Cadillac. Smith didn't like it and he found himself trying to see their hands. He slowly let off the brake to inch forward to use his door panels as cover should a fire fight ensue. The Cadillac also inched forward. They were taunting him. He disengaged the safety measures of his holster and unlocked the rifle holder. *If it's going down, I'm gonna take as many of these bastards I can with me.* His pulse accelerated. He wondered how long until the light turned green. *What's my escape route? Where are the third passenger's hands? Are they reaching under their seats? What's my backdrop?* All these thoughts raced through his mind as a bead of sweat ran from his forehead down into his cumbersome ballistic vest. He wondered if the expiration date was past due on the damn thing. *I'll check the date after my shift.*

A loud bang went off behind Smith and he nearly had a heart attack as he spun his head behind him to see where it came from. He saw an old Volkswagen bug and a yuppie grinning sheepishly. Smith whipped around to look for the Cadillac. It was gone. He looked up and the light was green. *Jesus, that was wild.* He was still in one piece, so he continued to the missing child call.

Smith met with the parents at the front door. The father's eyes bulged and he started gnawing on his fingernails at the sight of Smith. Smith found it odd that the man was so freaked out by his presence. He tried to be professional, but this was the third time this family had called for service. Each time he responded he found the missing daughter with her seventeen-year-old boyfriend. Smith finally figured out that the missing child's family wants the Sheriff's Office to do *their* job...raise their child.

They say their daughter is out of control and won't listen to them. Smith, during the course of his investigation of said child, had contacted the child's school. The school felt the same as him...the family wants the school to raise *their* child. She received stellar grades, was involved with school activities and sports, and she volunteered time to help the homeless-far from incorrigible in Smith's eyes.

"Can I come in?" Smith asked the father. The man shook his head and kept looking at Smith's firearm. He didn't answer. Smith had detected something wasn't right, but he wasn't sure what.

He dug further. *What's really going on here?* Something about the case and the way the mother looked at him concerned him. The father seemed paranoid and kept looking down the hallway like he was waiting for someone to come from a room. He made a few phone calls and located the missing child...she was at school, where she was supposed to be. *The only thing missing is the parents,* he thought.

Smith was frustrated because he felt the family was playing him and the Sheriff's Office. He had two calls for service pending now, and he was stuck dealing with a call that really wasn't a call.

"Look, I'm not sure what to tell you guys. She's at school and you knew it. Why'd you report her missing?" Smith was trying to read their faces, get a sense of what the hell was really going on.

The father looked at the mother, she turned away, and he looked back at Smith. He looked down the hall again and back at Smith. He looked at Smith's firearm and back down the hallway. The hair on the back of Smith's neck spiked. *Uh oh.*

"Come on guys. What's up, and what's down the hall?" Smith said to them while pointing down the hallway.

The mother began to shake and the father looked like he'd seen a ghost.

Smith walked toward the hallway. The mother trembled and the father shuffled in front of him. He towered over the father and physically moved him out of the way.

"There's nothing! You can't go down there. You need a search warrant to search my house," the father said in an almost robotic tone. Smith noticed the man was terrified. He had seen that look before, and now he was asking for a cover unit on the radio.

Smith peeked in the first room, nothing out of the ordinary. The mother was sobbing and the father continued to plead. "Stop, you can't go down there!" Smith forged on. He checked the bathroom and the closet and saw nothing.

A hysterical scream from the mother caused Smith to shudder and then he heard it...a loud thump that came from the last room. The door was closed and he grabbed the handle. It was locked from the outside. The father was shaking now...he was white like a corpse. He stood near the kitchen with a blank look on his face.

"Give me the key, or I break the door down," Smith growled. The father didn't respond, but continued to shake his head. Every fiber in Smith's body told him something bad was behind the door. He heard a siren close by. It was time to act.

"I called! I called, he's in there," the mother whined while fleeing out the front door.

Without hesitation, Smith shouldered the door and barreled into the room. He saw the seventeen-year-old boyfriend gagged and bounded to a chair that had fallen over. *The thud!* The visual and what it meant registered in Smith's mind. He spun and pulled his firearm then bang! In the blink of an eye, he lost his hearing and immense pressure pushed him to the floor. Two more loud bangs followed during the confusion.

Smith looked up to see the father standing in front of him. He was holding a gun and time had slowed way down. The gun slipped to the floor and Smith saw bullet holes covered in blood in the father's chest. The man slumped over and his lifeless body made a sick gurgling sound after hitting the floor revealing Beefcake standing in the doorway- smoke still lingered from his duty weapon. Smith cracked a wry smile. He unbuttoned his shirt and saw the ballistic vest had caught the bullet fired at his chest by the father.

"Damn Beefcake, next time leave her house a little quicker," he said with a grin and wink after noticing Beefcake's uniform was un-tucked and lipstick was on his collar.

Contributor Biographies:

Sunny Frazier: After working 17 years with the Fresno Sheriff's Department, 11 spent as Girl Friday with an undercover narcotics team, it dawned on Sunny Frazier that mystery writing was her real calling. All three of her novels in the Christy Bristol Astrology Mysteries are based on actual cases with a bit of astrology added, a habit Frazier has developed over the past 42 years.

Harriet Fox: Harriet Fox is a seasoned veteran in the law enforcement field and has worked a myriad of positions during almost twenty years of service. She's an inspiring author with a featured column on www.correctionsone.com and has a great passion for her work. She's intrigued by crime and mystery, loves life, but is looking forward to retirement.

Nick Perna: Nick Perna is a Sergeant with the Redwood City Police Department in Northern California. He has spent much of his career as a gang and narcotics investigator. He is a member of a Multi-Jurisdictional SWAT Team since 2001 and is currently a Team Leader. He previously served as a paratrooper in the US Army and is a veteran of Operation Iraqi Freedom. He has a Master's Degree from the University Of San Francisco.

Denise Spiller: Denise is a law enforcement professional in the San Francisco Bay Area. Read more about her at http://www.neceewrites.wordpress.com

Rick Tippins: Rick has served 23 years in law enforcement covering almost every capacity his employer offers to the community. Assignments have ranged from undercover narcotics to investigating murders. In his off time, he enjoys ice hockey and spending time with my family. He loves screen writing and dabbles in short stories.

Jay Padar: Jay Padar is currently a sergeant with the Chicago Police Department and has worked as a patrol officer and tactical officer. He has completed his 17th year with the department. Jay is a member of the Public Safety Writer's Association.

Jim Padar: Jim Padar was a Chicago Police Officer for 29 years, serving most of his street duty as a homicide detective. He finished his career serving as Operations Manager of the Chicago 911 system. He is a graduate of the 139th session of the FBI National Academy.

Sherrill Swinney: Sherrill Lee Swinney served in the United States Navy in Vietnam. He spends his time reading and writing while living in Florida. He's also the father of Chris Swinney.

Ian Snyder: Ian Snyder is an insurance professional who volunteers with the local Sheriff's office as a Posse man that patrols his local jurisdiction. Ian has been in law enforcement for almost five years and enjoys helping in his community.

Rick Smith: (DET.) Richard "Rick" Smith medically separated from police work in 2012. He still resides in

Ridgecrest Ca. with his wife Virginia and 3 kids. He currently teaches Criminal Justice at a local high school and Police Officer Training at the local college.

C.L.Swinney: Chris has been in law enforcement for over 15 years, ranging in assignments from Probation Officer to narcotics and homicide detective. He's written three best-selling crime fiction novels (The Bill Dix Series), an international best-selling true crime novel (Robert Pickton: The Pig Farmer Killer), and his short stories and poetry have been featured in several publications (Fly Fisherman Magazine, Chiron Review, and Conceit Magazine.

David Kettering: David Kettering is a Correctional Officer in a northern California county where he is currently assigned to the Jail Planning Bureau. Officer Kettering began his career in law enforcement 10 years ago as his fifth career after consulting meteorologist, semiconductor process engineer, marketing manager, and real estate loan officer. As was pointed out by one of his past co-workers,

Officer Kettering prefers to follow Robert Frost's advice...he takes the road less traveled. And that has made all the difference.

Made in the USA
Middletown, DE
21 August 2017